CONTENTS

A MASTER'S
SECRET WHISPERS

A Master's Secret Whispers

Dialogues between master and student about
The Secrets Of Life

A WORD BEFORE WE BEGIN

I could tell you that I've spent more than twenty five years studying the intricate nuances of the human mind . . .

I could tell you that there are many Truths about your life, your mind, and your path to experience that which you have craved since the freedom of your youth . . .

I could tell you that the society in which we live is awash in trite, prescriptive, and wholly ineffective methodologies aimed at the Unserious . . .

I could tell you that the greatest prison of your entire existence is the mind that you have been told to revere . . .

I could tell you that anxiety has a cure . . .
I could tell you that emotional pain has an identifiable source . . .
I could tell you that freedom will absolutely come to you if

you walk The Journey, after having cultivated the sincere and authentic desire to taste it . . .

There are so many things that I could tell you. Most of which your mind will not accept. And others which it will not understand. Not on account of ability or intelligence. But simply due to an innocent lack of exposure and never having been given the opportunity to experience The Experience.

I seek not to proselytize.

I seek not to convince.

What is written on these pages is an offering.

For the one who is ready to receive it.

Namaste.

MASTER, HOW DO I BELIEVE?

Student (S). Master (M).

S: Master, there is a question that I have wanted to ask you for a very long time. But I've never quite known how to ask it.

M: Speak freely, student.

S: Since I cannot formulate the words in a refined way, I shall just express to you my sentiments in their raw form.

M: That is the best way, my student.

S: Master, many of the things that you speak of to me and to those who come to you seem fantastical. They sound beautiful. And I am very taken by them. But sometimes they seem impractical to me. I suppose what I seek more than anything is to believe. As you believe.

M: This is a very sincere question, my student. It has the signs of coming straight from the heart. I am humbled to receive it. You must understand something very clearly, my student. I have no faith in belief. Nor do I subscribe to any belief. Either I Know, or I Do Not Know. But I do not "believe."

S: Then I seek to Know the things that you Know. But something tells me that when you say the word Know, you are not speaking of an intellectual sort of Knowing.

M: Your intelligence is keen, student. You are perfectly correct. To Know something intellectually is to never have known it at all.

S: And this is my quandary. The things that you speak of I am completely taken by. And I am taken by them in the heart. But I "know" them only in the head.

M: It must be so, student. For this is the way it begins for all human beings.

S: Even for you, Master?

M: Most certainly. Every man who becomes wise was once a fool. In the beginning, I too understood things on a purely intellectual level.

S: Then how did this intellectual understanding transform into a Knowing?

M: Shall I tell you precisely how it happens?

S: Yes, Master. Please.

M: It happens through a constant revisitation of the ideal that you wish to Know. A constant revisitation allows it to seep into one's bones. A constant revisitation allows one to Understand it from all angles. And that which was once Intellectual, in time becomes Experiential. And the space within oneself that was once occupied by The Mind, slowly becomes replaced by the Knowing. And the human being begins to Become the ideal that he so eagerly has revisited.

S: And how is this revisiting done, Master?

M: Nature gives nothing for Free, my student.

S: I do not understand.

M: The time is inappropriate for such a question, student. First you must find an ideal that you truly, truly wish to imbibe. An ideal that makes you shake. An ideal that literally brings tears to your eyes. For this will demonstrate your Authenticity for wanting to know it on more than simply an intellectual level.

S: I see.

M: You must understand, student, that most men have no interest in such depth. They trade and roam in the cosmetics of how's and wherefore's. They have no authentic longing for anything. They are interested only in window shopping. They seek to live their lives on safe and comfortable shores, never daring to drink the ocean.

S: And as for the practicality of such lofty ideals?

M: You must understand something, my student. Nothing in the world is practical unless it is first Non-negotiable.

S: Please explain, Master.

M: For a man who stands on the shore, diving into the depths of the ocean can never be practical. No methodology will suit him. For "practicality" is not meant for the Seeker. It is meant for the scientist. And it is only The Artist who tastes the nectar of life. The scientist tastes only the bitter chemicals found in test tubes.

S: Then how shall I proceed?

M: My student, the human being who is not swimming in Sincerity cannot ever be given a Way that is sufficiently practical for him. First he must dive into the depths, and Then learn the practicality of swimming.

S: One such Ocean of which I speak is Freedom. No matter how much I try, I cannot find it, Master.

M: You must first discover what you seek Freedom For and Freedom From. What is your personal definition of Freedom? What is it that you would like to happen to you? What does it look like? What does it feel like? You must answer many such questions. And you must examine your answers in order to see if they are of the Mind or of the Heart. How Insane are you for the things that you seek? How insane are you for this Freedom?

S: Yes, I must do precisely that.

M: You see, my student, every man speaks as you do. They speak of impracticality and difficulties and loftiness . . . But even the Impossible is made Possible by a man's Sincerity. Impossibility simply has no power in the face of Genuine Desire. None whatsoever. Every single man will have what he Insists upon having. And if he insists upon nothing in particular, he will live in the default and wayward musings of The Mind. Unless you are going Somewhere, you are going Nowhere. And even Nowhere is the Perfect place to go if you are <u>specifically</u> going Nowhere.

S: I have nothing to say, Master.

M: Impossibility will bow at your alter, my student. But first become a man worthy of being bowed to. Not through fame and accomplishment. But through Uncompromising Sincerity. Be not a pretender, my dear student. Be Uncompromising. For the man who refuses to compromise holds The Universe in his hands.

S: Thank you, my Master.

Master, He Has Defamed You

Student (S). Master (M).

S: Master, I have just returned from the village. Boga has said many things about you. Do you know this?

M: Yes.

S: Were you close to him, Master?

M: I have trained him since he was a boy.

S: He is saying terrible things about you. He says that he will no longer follow you. He says that you are an old fool. It is very difficult for me to hear, Master.

M: I understand, student.

S: He must be stopped. I was thinking that I might take two others and confront him.

M: That is not necessary.

S: Master, have you heard all of the things he has said about you?

M: Yes, they have been told to me in great detail.

S: What will you do?

M: About what, my student?

S: About Boga!

M: Am I to do something?

S: Are you not?

M: I was sitting in the garden today. And I saw an old fisherman. He walked down the North face of the mountain. I found that odd.

S: Excuse me, Master?

M: The Eastern face of the mountain is much flatter. I was wondering why he descended down the North face. And in leather sandals.

S: Are you avoiding me, Master?

M: No, my student. Why should I avoid you?

S: You have not answered my question about Boga.

M: I am far more interested in the fisherman.

S: But why?

M: Why not?

S: Master, does it not hurt you to know that a man who you have trained since he was a little boy is now defaming you to those who will hear him?

M: Hurt?

S: Yes, hurt.

M: (Laughs). What am I to do with hurt, my student? Why would I visit such a place?

S: Visit? You don't visit hurt. It visits you.

M: Hurt arises, my student. It does not visit.

S: And does it not arise in this case?

M: Very well. Call Boga to me, my student.

S: He may not come.

M: Tell him that I long to see him.

S: Yes, Master.

That afternoon, Boga arrived to see the Master. Master was sitting in the courtyard.

Boga: You called for me, Master?

M: Yes, Boga. Please come.

Boga: I take it you have heard what I have done.

M: Yes.

Boga: What do you want from me?

12

M: Have I ever wanted anything from you, my student?

Boga: I am not ashamed of the things I have said.

M: Nor should you be.

Boga: Then why have you summoned me, Master?

M: To apologize.

Boga: Apologize?

M: Yes, my student.

Boga: For what?

M: For what I have done to you.

Boga: What did you do to me?

M: I have wronged you terribly, Boga.

Boga: How so?

M: I do not know.

Boga: I do not understand, Master.

M: No man acts irrationally, my student. Each has a reason for his actions. He acts according to the will that arises within him. I do not know what I have done. And I do not need to know. But there is something that I most definitely have done to cause you to react this way against me.

Boga: You were strict and you did not understand me and you only answered questions in your time, not mine, and —

M: No need to tell me, my student. For I will correct them not.

Boga: I do not understand your words, Master.

M: I do not know what I have done. But I do know that my intentions toward you have always come from a place of Sincerity. I never allowed myself to bow to your mind. I sought only to free your heart. When a Master has such unwavering visions for his student, his ways will seem strange. And they rarely may incite reactions such as the ones that have arisen in you.

Boga: Then why do you seek to apologize?

M: Because for the briefest moment when I first heard the news,

I thought that you should not have done what you did. This thought flashed across my mind for not more than a second. But it arose nonetheless. And this suggests that my mind has not yet totally been eradicated.

Boga: Less than a second?

M: Yes.

Boga: Of what consequence is that? You quickly quelled it and continued on in serenity.

M: It matters not. It should never have arisen. And for this I would like to apologize to you, my student.

Boga: But what of the things that I did?

M: What one man does has no bearing on another. There is no relativism. No comparisons. There exists only IS and IS NOT.

Boga: Master, may I ask you a question?

M: Yes.

Boga: Does it trouble you that I might go on speaking about you in the way that I have been doing?

M: No, my student.

Boga: May I ask you one final question?

M: Yes, my student.

Boga: After all that has happened, why do you continue to respectfully call me your student?

M: Because after all that has happened my student, I am still learning how to best become your Master.

MASTER, PLEASE TELL ME THE SECRET TO SUCCESS

Student (S). Master (M).

S: Master, many try and fail. Yet some succeed. And others succeed royally. Why is this so?

M: There is something about success that even those who succeed do not understand.

S: What is that?

M: That it is a self-created drama.

S: How so?

M: Man spends so much of his time trying to "succeed" that he overlooks the things that will give it to him quite easily.

S: I do not understand.

M: You see, my student, the entire notion of "success" versus "failure" has become a thing of its own. Man has created a beast. And this beast called "success" has become completely independent of the thing that he wishes to succeed at.

S: What you are saying, then, is that one should not be interested in success?

M: It depends.

S: Upon what?

M: Upon the nature of the journey one wishes to have.

S: The nature of the journey, Master?

M: Indeed. If one seeks to have a peaceful journey, then he will have to understand some of the Truths. If he is drawn to the romanticism of striving for success and hard work, then he is the sort of man who is more interested in the "struggle."

S: Is any man interested in the struggle, Master?

M: Certainly.

S: Why would any man wish to struggle?

M: Because it is a romantic idea. It is fancy. It is "heroic."

S: And what you are saying is that success can be had without struggle?

M: Even You speak of "success" as a mythological and romantic ideal. Tell me student, what do you mean by "success?"

S: Let us take the legendary swordsman Miyamoto Musashi. In all his life, he never lost a battle. This is what any man would consider success. Success that is unparalleled in any land.

M: Very well. Do you know the back story of Musashi, my student?

S: No, Master. Only that he was the best that has ever lived.

M: Musashi devoted the whole of his days and nights to a study of not only the sword, but of the mind. In seclusion. In the depths of the jungle. It was not a striving, nor a struggle. He became a Master of the sword. While others did not.

S: And, therefore, Master?

M: And, therefore, he had no need to chase success. There was no success. There was no failure. He became the Supreme Master of the Sword. Of what use does such a man have to chase success?

S: A profound thought just came to me, Master. What you are essentially saying is that success is for the mediocre.

M: Few will understand the Great Truth that you have just spoken, my student. You are best to keep such things close to your chest.

S: But men would be helped by such knowledge, Master.

M: Search the kingdom and bring to me that man who is willing to imbibe it.

S: Master, then what is to be made of hard work and practice?

M: My dear student, if one has given the whole of himself to becoming a Master, he will do what is necessary to become it. And it will be a joy for him. It will be an intense journey. And peaceful the entire way. Hard work and practice are for those who try to become that which they secretly believe that it is difficult for them to become.

S: Thank you, my Master.

MASTER, HOW DO YOU LIVE IN EASE?

Student (S). Master (M).

S: Master, I watch the way in which you do things. I see the way you react to things. You do it all with complete ease. How is this possible?

M: Such things happen by themselves.

S: In what way?

M: How do you mean, student?

S: I find myself getting anxious in various situations. I worry about outcomes. I get perturbed by what people say.

M: Such things happen to you because you have not had the

21

necessary realizations.

S: What realizations are those, Master?

M: You may think me difficult, but if I were to answer this question directly it would do little for you.
S: Why, Master?

M: Because if I simply tell you to understand this and to know that . . . If I tell you that such and such is the way things are, you may hear me, but in many ways the words will pass you by.

S: Do you think I will not understand them?

M: You will understand their dictionary meaning. But you will not understand their depth.

S: I see.

M: Understand, my dear student, that anxiety is a byproduct. It cannot be eliminated head-on. One must penetrate the source from which it arises.

S: And what is that source?

M: The source is the failure to realize that which must be realized.

In the heart. Never in the head.

S: It seems fantastical to live completely without anxiety.

M: Many things will seem fantastical to you, student. They will seem a thousand miles away. There are things that a man was meant to experience that most would relegate to the realm of magic and fantasy. But, in fact, magic and fantasy are at the heart of man's existence.

S: Then why does he not live in this way? Why does he not live a magical life?

M: How can he?

S: How do you mean, Master?

M: Man lives in a world whose noise is so wide and deep that it requires either an extraordinary DNA or a cataclysmic chance occurrence for him to turn away from the noise and seek The Truth. It is almost impossible for him to deem that all that he has been told for his entire life and all that he hears on a daily basis is completely false and full of lies. Monumentally rare are such men. But this is the only way. For without it, one is destined to a life of misery, turmoil, and anxiety.

S: You are saying that man is doomed?

M: From the standpoint of his birthright, he is not. From the standpoint of what is possible for him, he is not. But from the standpoint of the likelihood and practicality of his turning against all the noise of the world and seek a way out of his mind, yes he is almost certainly doomed.

S: Is nature not cruel in this way, Master?

M: I do not have an answer for you, my student. I can only say that The Truth and The Path does not come to a man by accident. One must have an overwhelming and genuine desire to live a life of Freedom and completely free of turmoil. Or he simply will not have it. And if he dares to think in such a way, society will tell him that such things are, as you say, "magic and fantasy."

S: There is much for me to learn.

M: If your desire is genuine, learning will come. All things come by way of Sincerity.

S: And I suppose it was your sincere desire to live a life of ease?

M: It was my sincere desire to know The Truth about all things. The absolute, undeniable, ultimate Truth. I knew that The Truth

24

would lead to such a life.

S: Anxiety, thus, never touches you, Master?

M: Never do I give birth to its possibility, my student. And if one does not give birth to something, how can it possibly arise?

S: Thank you, my Master.

MASTER, PLEASE SPEAK ABOUT PARENTING

Student (S). Master (M).

S: Master, you are a parent, are you not?

M: I was once.

S: You do not have children?

M: I do.

S: Then you are still a parent.

M: I have children. But I am no longer a parent.

S: Have you disavowed your children?

M: Quite the contrary.

S: I do not understand, Master.

M: When a human being gets a child, something very interesting happens. He becomes cast into a role of a parent. And this is not a role that he is ready for.

S: Why not?

M: Understand this: A psychologist never truly sees the human being who walks into her office. She sees only a Patient. She sees herself as a psychologist, and thus the only thing in the world that she is able to see the other person as is a Patient. This destroys all possibility of human connection. She is playing a role. And thus she has no choice but to place the person who comes to her into a role. It is the same with a parent. A parent sees the child as His Child. He does not see the child as a human being. And thus it is doomed from the beginning.

S: But the child is indeed His Child.

M: Every parent thinks that this is the case. But, in truth, it is not.

S: Why not?

M: The child is an entity independent of the parent. He belongs to Nature. He does not belong to the Parent. Every parent is a surrogate. Nature uses the parent to bear the child. But it does not grant her ownership of him.

S: What is wrong with ownership?

M: That which a man Owns, he destroys.

S: Did you also look upon your children in this way?

M: Yes. Until wisdom began to dispel my ignorance.

S: How do you view your children now, Master?

M: In order for me to see them, I first had to eliminate the role of "parent." It is only once I stepped out of this role, that seeing them became possible.

S: And once you did, what did you see?

M: My dear student, I saw all that I had missed throughout their early years. I saw that these children were being raised by a fool. For he did not see them at all. He saw only himself. When I relinquished the role of parent, I began to see the magic within them. I began to see the possibilities within them. I began to see the things that they had that I did not. And I remember the day I dropped to my knees in reverence and apology. A child does not deserve a "parent." He deserves freedom from one.

S: I do not know what to say, Master.

M: Understand, my student. When you place yourself into a role, you can only see the other through the eyes of that role. When you have no role, you begin to see the flesh and blood human being. Where I once parented my children, I now revere them. Where I once taught them, I now learn from them. And is it not the height of irony, that they now listen to my every word, when I no longer need them to listen.

S: Thank you, my Master.

MASTER, WHAT IS YOUR LIFE LIKE?

Student (S). Master (M).

S: Master, I watch you. I see you. I examine the way in which you do things. But what is your life like from the inside? From inside of you?

M: My life is like the snowflake. It falls with the freedom of falling. Knowing that when it lands it will feel no pain. Because the moment it touches the ground, it will melt.

S: I do not know what to say, Master. Can you please explain more?

M: My life is like the leaf that trembles and changes color according to the seasons. Not knowing or caring that it has done so.

S: Continue please.

M: My life is like the Eagle that soars across the great blue sky. With no place, in particular, to go.

S: More, please.

M: My life does not move. It has too much weight to move. It never leaves the moment. For it cannot survive outside of it.

S: How did it come to take such splendid form, Master? You must tell me. For today you have rendered me speechless.

M: It did not happen by accident.

S: Then how did all of this happen to you?

M: If I may be honest with you, my student, I will say that I do not know what possesses a man to have such sensibilities. I do not know why one man seeks such a life, and another does not. I can only say that to live such a life was bound to happen for me.

S: Bound to happen?

M: With certainty.

S: Why?

M: As I have mentioned to you before, I lived in ignorance for many years. However, there existed within me a deep and profound desire to Know. And an insistence to Truly Live. And I knew that because of the Sincerity of my desire, the universe would send someone to me in order to guide me to the life I have described.

S: And it did?

M: It had no choice.

S: And this someone that the universe sent to you was your Master?

M: Yes.

S: What is it that you learned from him?

M: Everything, my dear student. Everything.

S: Life from your eyes has no pain, is this correct?

M: My life no longer has pain. This is correct. There is no turmoil in the least. In fact, my life happens as I wish it to happen.

S: But, my Master, even learned men say that no man's life happens as he likes it.

M: This is true for the vast majority of human beings. But then there are the few to whom life suspends its will and bows to the man himself.

S: What you are saying is that there IS a way.

M: Indeed.

S: But you will not tell it to me.

M: The Way is not a map, my student.

S: Then what is it?

M: The way is revealed without being revealed.

S: I do not understand, my Master.

M: It is very difficult to explain. But understand this, The Way is only possible as an alchemy. And it takes birth the moment that a student gives the whole of his heart to the One Who Knows.

S: Have I not given the whole of my heart to you, Master?

M: You have given me a few strategic and calculated fragments, my student. But it is very important that you do not take this as a challenge or a motivation to give it all to me. For then it will not be authentic. When you are truly ready to live such a life, you will give all of it to me. When nothing on the whole of this Earth matters more to you, you will surrender it with open hands and soft eyes.

S: You put me to shame, Master. Please tell me how you feel on a daily basis.

M: Each thing for me isn't a thing. It is like a slow adventure. When the water runs through the faucet it feels like a remote African waterfall. Each step is taken lightheartedly, with an almost wistful anticipation of the texture of ground that it is about to experience. There is no longer a series of things. There is no longer a number of events. For me, there is only THIS.

S: This?

M: Yes, THIS. THIS is my entire world. THIS is my solid foundation. THIS is my entire life. If you were to cut my life open longitudinally, you would find only THIS.

S: What profound things you have learned, Master. Your words shake the very ground beneath my feet.

M: Man spends the whole of his life searching for things that do not exist. This is the fate of almost every man on this Earth. May I promise you something?

S: Please, my Master.

M: Though, as you say, my words have shaken the very ground beneath your feet, moments after this exchange you will return to a life of enslavement. You will have all but forgotten about this exchange.

S: I will not, Master. This I can assure you.

M: (Smile). As you say, my student.

MASTER, WHY DO THESE PEOPLE COME TO YOU?

Student (S). Master (M).

S: Master, I see men come to you from far and wide. Dressed in suits and flanked by assistants and security guards. I've seen them present you with large sums of money and gifts. Sometimes even cars. Why do they do this?

M: How is it that you know this, student?

S: I watch in secret, Master. I could ask you to forgive me but I would be lying if I did. For I am amazed at this sight. And I cannot promise that I will not do it again.

M: Honesty has a home in you. You need not apologize.

S: What do these men seek from you, Master?

M: Do you ask in passing? Or do you wish to know the Truth?

S: The truth, Master.

M: The truth is, they do not know what they seek.

S: If they do not know what they seek, why do they pay you royally and present you with gifts?

M: Understand, my student. When I say to you that men do not know what they seek, you think it odd. Your mind tells you that if a man is willing to "pay royally" as you put it, then he must know exactly what he is seeking in return. Is this correct?

S: Yes indeed, Master.

M: May I ask you a question, student?

S: Yes, Master.

M: What is it that you seek?

S: I seek many things, Master.

M: Many things?

S: Yes, many things.

M: But all things are related. They are intertwined. The man who seeks many things has not found the root which affects them all.
S: Is this so, Master?

M: There is no "many," my dear student. There is only One.

S: Only one thing?

M: I can see your mind tumbling to a fall. Your mind is now examining the "many" things as we speak. And it is trying to choose between them.

S: You are correct, Master. How do you know this?

M: It matters not how I know, student. What matters is that you do not know what precisely you seek. Is this not so?

S: You are correct, Master. I must be honest. I do not know the one thing upon which all others rest.

M: Your humility is lovely to witness. As for these men who come to me, they are the Princes of the Earth.

S: Truly?

M: Truly.

S: How so, if you do not mind me asking.

M: The overwhelming majority of men live a deplorable life, my student. I am intimate with just how deplorable it is, for there was a time that I too lived in this way. My life had no Peace. The mind ran and ran and ran. Endless thoughts bombarded my waking existence. And in the night they turned into uncontrollable dreams. My life was essentially a series of events. A series of chores. And endless monotony of "doings." One after the other. An endless list of worries. Emotion would routinely get the better of me. Uncertainty would be my companion. Shall I continue?

S: I feel many of these things myself, Master. Please continue.

M: These men who come to me also feel these things. They do not know precisely what they seek. But they seek a way out of this. And for this, they are the Princes of the Earth.

S: Please forgive me, but I still do not understand why they are the Princes of the Earth.

M: Because almost all men in the world live such a life. And they die in its grips. It is not only that they do not take action to seek a way out. They do not even recognize that they live in turmoil. They

39

do not even see it. They believe that this is the way it was supposed to be. They believe that this is all there is. They believe that nothing beyond this misery, strife, and turmoil exists. They say things like, "that's life." And if one does not even suspect that something beyond all of this even exists, why would he seek help for a way out?

S: I see.

M: But these men that you speak of have had the insight, either through Grace or Karma to suspect that there must be a Way. They believe that glory must exist. They cannot allow themselves to accept that their current way of living is all there is. And thus they come. And this one insight and the steps they take to seek help is what separates them from the bulk of humanity. This is why they are the Princes of the Earth. And this is why I respect them.

S: You have opened my eyes, Master. I will confess that I thought myself better than these men. But now I realize that I am one of them.

M: You are very wise, my student. Men who seek The Truth are as rare as the rarest gem. They come to me and tell me that, at last, they have found me. But what they do not realize is that I, at last, have found them.

S: Thank you, my Master.

MASTER, HOW DID YOU BECOME THE GREATEST?

Student (S). Master (M).

S: Master, I have watched your skill at archery. And the spear. And the sword. And all men concur that there is no one greater than you in the land. How did you come to be the greatest?

M: There is a story behind this, student.

S: Please tell me, Master.

M: There was a time when I was feeble. And would cower at the sight of battle. My skill was that of a strict novice. And there was no greatness to speak of.

S: Everyone begins this way, Master.

M: I think not.

S: How so?

M: Talent is a real thing. And although I had it, I could not wield it.

S: Why?

M: I was ignorant in the manner of battle. And I was not learned in the majesty of the mind.

S: Please tell me more, Master.

M: Many times I went into battle with more skill than my opponent. But I had no chance.

S: Why?

M: My student, possessing something is one thing. Having access to it is another.

S: I do not understand, Master.

M: In those days, I worked long and hard to develop my skill. But it remained locked away. For I was prey to the greed of winning. And this greed of winning led me into the bowels of fear. And a fearful man cannot fight. He can only flail.

S: How did you come through this, Master?

M: I learned, my student. I learned.

S: What did you learn?

M: Allow me to say this, as I want it to reach your heart. Precisely what I learned I will share with you in a moment. But I want you to understand something firmly and clearly.

S: Yes, Master?

M: A willingness to learn is rare among men. Men are predisposed to "do." Few among them are willing and ready to Learn.

S: I am listening, Master.

M: Because I was willing to finally learn, I finally began to listen to my Master. For years he had tried to teach me, but the rarest thing in all the world is a Genuine Student.

S: What did your Master teach you?

M: He taught me many things. But it was only once I had the ears to hear them that they penetrated my heart. My skill was locked away because of ego. And an egoistic man cannot learn.

S: How does ego lock a man's skill?

M: Because the egoistic man views battle as a contest. And thus he becomes limited.

S: I do not understand, Master.

M: What you must understand, my student, is that "incremental betterment" and "inching past the other" instantly relegates a man into struggle. He may have attained the heavens. But because his eyes are fixed upon the other, he barely attains the low hanging limb of the willow.

S: I see.

M: One must understand what it is he wishes to achieve. He must understand precisely why it is that he fights. And his vision must be greater than the greatest who have come before him. In order to take himself and his craft to a level it would not have reached without him.

S: How, then, did your way in battle change?

M: I attained what every warrior wishes, but few imagine as possible.

S: What is that?

M: Freedom in battle.

S: Freedom.

M: Yes, Freedom. And when I became free, my skill was unleashed. I could wield it without consequence. I was beyond the grasp of fear. For I had learned The Truth.

S: You have inspired me, Master. I too wish to learn The Truth.

M: Yes. I can see it in your eyes.

S: Let us begin. Now!

M: I will begin with this: Do not roam among the haggard and the meek. Do not fight for scraps of food that are moist with stagnant rains. Do not enter the crucible of egoistic men who compete over dime and dollar. Rise, my student. And insist First upon the glory of Freedom. So that no arena can contain you. And no man can equal you. For your journey is unlike any other man in the field.

S: Thank you, my Master.

MASTER, HOW CAN I NOT CARE?

Student (S). Master (M).

S: Master, you do not seem to care about much of anything.

M: How do you know this?

S: I can see it in your manner.

M: Yes, what of it?

S: I also seek not to care.

M: Why?

S: Because not caring is freedom, Master.

M: A wise statement indeed.

46

S: Please tell me, Master. How is it that I too can come to the point in which I no longer care?

M: One comes upon it through understanding, my student.

S: Understanding what?

M: Understanding the way of things. Understanding the patterns of the mind.

S: Please tell me more, Master.

M: You ask a very odd question. But also one that is at the essence of wisdom.

S: I seek it deeply, Master.

M: What is it that you wish not to care about?

S: What is it that You do not care about, Master?

M: What do you think?

S: I think that you care not about anything.

M: It is so.

S: I too wish to be like that.

M: Then you will have to let go of something that is very dear to you.

S: What is that, Master?

M: Happiness.

S: But not caring makes you happy, does it not?

M: No.

S: Then what does not caring give you, if not happiness?

M: Freedom.

S: Yes, freedom! I want freedom!

M: Then you first must learn to be free of happiness.

S: Are you free of happiness?

M: Yes. And I can see that you have already begun to resist.

S: But why do you not seek to be happy?

M: Because happiness is for fools.

S: Do you then seek to be miserable, Master?

M: Miserable is what a man becomes when he hankers for happiness.

S: I am confused.

M: Why?

S: Because I do not know what to do.

M: Why did you create such a conundrum for yourself by asking such a heavy question?

S: Because I am fascinated by your lack of caring. It is enormously appealing to me.

M: I have come upon it through years of pain, heartache, misery, and ignorance.

S: Will I too come upon it, Master?

M: I do not know.

S: You do not wish to encourage me, I suppose.

M: Have I ever encouraged you, student?

S: No. What is the wisdom behind that, Master?

M: I do not know that there is wisdom behind it. I have no idea if it is right or wrong. I simply fail to see the point in doing so.

S: Is it that you wish for me to become tough?

M: You give me too much credit, student. I am more innocent than clever.

S: Master, may I ask you a question?

M: Yes.

S: You do not seem to care about anything. Do you care about me?

M: Care is an inappropriate word. You must forgive me but I left that word behind long ago.

S: Then what is your relationship with me?

M: Student, if you wish to learn, then learn. If you do not, then do not. But I will not imprison myself by the hope that you will.

S: And what of emotional attachment?

M: Emotional attachment comes out of the need for happiness.

S: What of the emotional attachment and caring that exists between a parent and child.

M: My student, you are not ready for the answer to such a question. For I can sense by the way that you are asking it that you are mildly horrified by what I might say. Let us leave that question to the wind.

S: Then tell me this, Master. What precisely is the freedom that not caring grants you?

M: The freedom from Need.

S: Thank you, my Master.

MASTER, HOW DO I FIND TRUTH?

Student (S). Master (M).

S: Master, I've heard you speak often of Truth. We are told many things by many people. The mind also tells us many things. How is it that I can know what is The Truth?

M: It cannot be arrived at purely by the intellect.

S: Then what is the way to recognize it?

M: You see, my student, The Truth is like a dagger. When it strikes you, it does something to you. The same way that a man says "ouch" and reacts to something painful. In the same way, when The Truth strikes a man, something within him reacts to it in a particular way. Almost like a Eureka moment. You will often hear him say things such as, "That feels right," or "That really hits home," or simply, "Yes!"

S: I can recall such feelings. But how does one come upon it in the first place?

M: The Truth is available to few men and also to all men.

S: How so, Master?

M: It is available to all men as a birthright. But only a few men exercise their birthright.

S: Why would a man not exercise his birthright?

M: What you are essentially asking is why one man is in love with finding The Truth, and another is not. I can only surmise that there is something within one man's constitution that is perhaps absent in his neighbor's. But I must confess that this is an imperfect answer, my student.

S: It is perplexing.

M: It is of little consequence for our purposes, my student. For there are enough men in the world who seek The Truth, and thus our halls will be selective, but certainly not empty.

S: But why do you think it is so?

M: My dear student, why does one man devote his life to climbing Everest, while another doesn't dare to leave his province? Why does one man seek to conquer the self, while another seeks to conquer the world? Why does one man seek to know Everything, while another is content with knowing what the world tells him? I apologize that I cannot provide you with a sincere answer to such questions, my student. I only know that it is so.

S: For the man who seeks it, how does it come to him?

M: Men who seek Truth have always been this way. If they look back into their childhood, they will find that they were Truth Seekers even then, in some form or fashion. Nature has a way of giving man exactly what he desires.

S: Is this so, Master?

M: Yes, my student, it is indeed so. Nature sees directly into our hearts. And it places us in circumstances and situations which serve to fulfill our True desire. It serendipitously sends people to us who have what we seek. It appears "coincidental" but I have lived long enough to know that coincidence is myth. All things are by design, my dear student. All things are by design.

S: What you are, then, saying is that if a man seeks it he shall have it?

M: If the quest is Genuine, he cannot help but to have it. It has always been so.

S: What of toil?

M: There is toil for the sake of toil. And there is toil that is fundamentally an exploration.

S: Kindly explain.

M: Imagine there are two men who are digging for water in different parts of a desert. One man digs because he has heard that if he digs, he might find water. Another man digs because the water that exists beneath the desert is something that he must find even if it kills him. From the outside, both toil. But one man's toil is a toil for toil's sake. While the other man's toil is the centerpiece of his life.

S: And toil for toil's sake is not good?

M: It is not a matter of good and bad, my student. The man who toils for toils sake does so only to satisfy himself that he has "toiled," as the world as told him to do. And if he does not find Truth, he is content to say that he did the necessary toil and still did not find it, and thus it wasn't meant to be.

S: Then what you are saying is that Truth is a fundamentally different journey.

M: Yes, my wise student. Truth is a journey of the heart. And the Truth is bestowed upon a man by whisper or messenger.

S: Thus one cannot cheat. Is this not so?

M: Nature is wiser than you think, my student. It tends to see through a man's words.

S: One must be willing to explore. Is this it?

M: The Seeker Of Truth cannot help but to explore, my student. For him there is no choice. And because he has no choice but to find it, nature has no choice but to grant it.

S: Thank you, my Master.

MASTER, WHAT IS AN INFERIORITY COMPLEX?

Student (S). Master (M).

S: Master, I sometimes feel inferior whilst sitting in a group of people. Why is this so?

M: For you to recognize this is most promising. For you to verbalize it is most impressive.

S: Please tell me The Truth about this, Master.

M: Most men feel inferior, my student.

S: Why?

M: You say you want The Truth, is it?

S: Yes, Master. Only The Truth.

M: The thing about The Truth is that it is often not understood by mortal ears, my student. The Truth in a particular thing may exist on a level 9 of complexity. And if the man to whom it is being told has not the understanding of the first 8 levels, he will not understand it.

S: Such things rarely seem to stop you, Master. Whether I understand it or not, I would like to bathe in it. For I would rather understand 3 percent of the truth, than 100% of that which is false.

M: Most impressive. If you would like to understand The Truth about this, then hear this my wise and courageous student: Man feels inferior because he lives from the standpoint of his personality.

S: You said I would not understand. And you are correct. But I humbly ask you to clarify.

M: You see, my student, when a man lives As his personality, he is limited. And something within him recognizes that his personality is limited. And thus he must say and do things in order to make up for the deficiencies that he feels himself to possess.

S: I see.

M: Yes. In the midst of others, he will find himself needing to say things that pad his own image. He will feel the need to say things that will heighten his importance in the eyes of others.

S: Please go on, Master.

M: Understand, my student, that even the most casual meetings of men exist within an undercurrent of competitiveness. Each attempting subtle and clever ways to display verbiage and mannerisms in order to quell their inner feelings of ineptitude.

S: If I am to be perfectly honest, I must confess that I do indeed feel these things that you speak of.

M: Almost all men share in your plight, my student.

S: You say, "almost."

M: Yes, my student. Almost.

S: Who are these men who do not?

M: The ones who no longer gain satisfaction from playing the game.

S: How is it that such men came to such a point in their lives, Master?

M: Because of an overwhelming desire to know The Truth. So that they could live Uncompromisingly Free.

S: That sounds lovely, my Master.

M: I sense hesitation in your voice.

S: It is just that . . . I do not know how to live as anything besides my personality.

M: I see.

S: Will you not help me, my Master?

M: May I ask you a question, my student?

S: Certainly, Master.

M: You say that you do not know how to live as anything besides a personality. What was your purpose in making such a statement?

S: You never compromise, do you.

M: Explain.

S: You do not allow me my indulgences.

M: To waste a minute is to waste a life, my student. I believe you have already answered my question. But please complete the thought so that I may be certain.

S: The reason that I said I do not know how to live as a personality is because I expected you to come to my rescue.

M: Indeed. And the reason that you seek to be rescued is because living in Uncompromising Freedom is perhaps not a desire that has yet taken hold of you.

S: But oh how I seek it to take hold of me, Master.

M: If your desire is genuine, it shall be so, my student.

S: How will you know when it has taken hold of me, my Master?

M: The nature of your questions will change. And the person who will be asking them will be someone other than the one who asks them now.

S: Thank you, my Master.

MASTER, WHAT IS MASTERY?

Student (S). Master (M).

S: Master, I often find it difficult to control the sword. One might explain that by saying that I am just a student. But even the Masters of neighboring sects do not seem to be any match for you. How is it that you wield the sword with such perfection?

M: What is the answer that you would like to hear, my student?

S: I do not understand, Master.

M: When human beings ask a question, they are in hopes of receiving a certain type of answer. One that fits with their own view of things.

S: I am confused, Master.

M: If I said to you that I worked harder than the other Masters, would that satisfy the thirst of your question?

S: Perhaps. But I also see the other Masters work quite hard.

M: Very well. And if I said that my technique was better than theirs, would that satisfy you?

S: I suppose I would fail to understand how someone who had been practicing for over thirty years could have an inferior technique.

M: Your words demonstrate wisdom, my student.

S: I truly seek to know, my Master.

M: Would you agree that any man who does something in a way that is superior to others knows something that they do not?

S: Yes. What is it that you know that the other Masters and I do not?

M: I know the power of Instinct.

S: And they do not?

M: They may know it. But they have not fallen in love with it.

S: How is it that you came to fall in love with instinct, Master?

M: Nature is perfect. And that is why I love nature. Instinct belongs to nature. And so I love it, as well.

S: And how does it serve you in battle, Master?

M: It is able to do things that I am not.

S: The other Masters do not know this?

M: There is knowing, and there is Knowing. There is knowing, and there is Loving.

S: Please explain, Master.

M: A man who brings his Instinct to battle will always have IT. A man who brings only his technique may have it or he may not.

S: Why is it that you know this and the other Masters do not?

M: I cannot say that they do not know this, my student. After all, they are Masters.

S: And yet you have prowess over them in wielding the sword.

M: As I said, there is knowing, and there is Loving. I Love instinct. I would not so much as walk to the garden without it.

S: I see.

M: Yes, my student. It is my trusted companion. It is the only thing I have ever been able to rely upon. For it has always served me. And it has served me well.

S: And what of hard work, Master?

M: I suppose I would say that "work" is perhaps best spent getting in touch with your instinct. To crawl inside of it. To become intimate with it. So that it may serve you as it has served me.

S: Thank you, my Master.

MASTER, WHAT IS THE SECRET TO CONFIDENCE?

Student (S). Master (M).

S: Master, there are many things about which I feel unsure of myself.

M: I see.

S: How can I become more certain?

M: I do not understand your question, student. Perhaps you could be more specific.

S: When I am in a group of people, I sometimes feel inferior. When I do some things, I feel unconfident about how well I will be able to do them.

M: You have raised a very ubiquitous and most delicate issue, my student. I applaud your vulnerability.

S: Thank you, Master.

M: You feel inferiority because you have fallen for the false game, my student.

S: The false game?

M: Yes. The false game is to give legitimacy to the notion that there is a hierarchy of importance among human beings.

S: But Master, such a thing does exist. There are important people in this world. And there are those who are not as important. And lest you tell me that all men are of equal importance, I will point out that some men are heralded by the masses. While no one heralds the masses themselves.

M: You are correct, my student. No one heralds the masses. For it is only the Unique and the Uncommon that are heralded. But as for "importance," I do not subscribe to this designation.

S: Why, Master?

M: Because nothing in this life is "important," my student.

S: Why do you say such a thing, my Master?

M: If a man who is born is sure to one day die, what could possibly be of any "importance?" How can something that is fleeting carry any importance at all, my student?

S: How does this relate to confidence, Master?

M: If you create a category called "importance" you will naturally be compelled to populate this category. And then you will be compelled to create a hierarchy of "importance." Following which you will find yourself with the difficult task of placing yourself somewhere within this hierarchy. And the moment you place yourself within this hierarchy, you will have created a problem.

S: How so, Master?

M: Because you will then suffer the weight of the hierarchy that sits above you.

S: But doesn't every man put himself at the highest level of importance?

M: If that is what you did, why would you have a problem with confidence?

S: I do not know, Master.

M: If you place yourself at the top, you will suffer the desperation of attempting to validate that position. And if you put yourself anywhere but the top, you will suffer the turmoil of having to reach a higher position. There is anxiety in both directions. For you are playing a game that you cannot win.

S: Then what should I do, Master?

M: Perhaps you can stop creating problems for yourself.

S: Is it wrong, then, to want to be confident?

M: Confidence, my student, is not a product of comparison. It is a product of indifference.

S: How so, Master?

M: If you are indifferent to what others think or believe about you, confidence will be with you.

S: How do I become indifferent, Master?

M: Why are you not indifferent already, my student?

S: I suppose I want to be thought highly of. And also liked and appreciated.

M: Then you will be an actor on a stage. Playing a role for the audience. In hopes of garnering an applause.

S: Do you not like applause, Master?

M: On the path to Wisdom, it is first imperative to let go of the "good." For only then is it possible to let go of the "bad."

S: But letting go of the "good" is to deny ourselves happiness, Master.

M: Indeed it is. If you fall for the trap of happiness, then you will forever be its slave.

S: So I should not seek applause. Nor should I seek to be liked or accepted?

M: There is no should.

S: Is this your recommendation?

M: I speak only The Truth, my dear student. I explain the way that things Truly Are. How you wish to proceed is your choice entirely.

S: So what you are saying is that once I become indifferent to the thoughts and feelings of others, confidence will not be an issue for me?

M: Yes.

S: But will my becoming indifferent to the thoughts and feelings of others not make me a heartless stone?

M: Quite the contrary. But just to humor you, may I ask you a question?

S: Yes, Master.

M: Would you rather be a heartless stone? Or an emotional wreck?

S: Are you certain I would be a heartless stone if I became indifferent?

M: You would not be a heartless stone by becoming indifferent. For the indifference would be a product of having learned.

S: Having learned what, my Master?

M: The indifference would be the product of you having learned that nothing really matters in this life. When a man understands this, indifference is the natural byproduct.

S: If nothing matters, then why should a man do anything at all, Master?

M: He doesn't need to do anything. But if he chooses to do something, let it be for the purpose of Truly Experiencing It, rather than doing it for "meaning" and "purpose."

S: So I shall speak freely in all conversations, Master?

M: Certainly. But do not try to convince anyone.

S: Why not?

M: If you try to convince someone, you are playing the false game. For the only reason you will be trying to convince them is in order to demonstrate the importance of your beliefs. But there is no importance at all.

S: So if I am asked a question, shall I speak the unflinching Truth as I see it, without any regard whatsoever for how that person might take it?

M: Yes.

S: And if he doesn't agree?

M: My dear student, if you speak The Truth, only a handful will agree.

S: And the rest?

M: The rest will think you Mad. And understand this, my dear student. The madman has no need whatsoever to acquire confidence. For he is never without it.

S: Thank you, my Master.

MASTER, WHAT IS INTELLIGENCE?

Student (S). Master (M).

S: Master, you will think me odd for asking this question. But what is intelligence?

M: Why should I think you odd, my student?

S: Because in asking 'what is intelligence' I seem to be implying that I am not.

M: And what is the trouble with implying that you are not?

S: I honestly do not know, my Master.

M: Is it that you feel I will look upon you as less than you are?

S: Perhaps.

74

M: Then your idea of intelligence is different from mine.

S: How so, Master?

M: For you, intelligence is something that you "possess." As if intelligence were the contents, and you the container.

S: Is this not the case, Master?

M: No, my student. This is not True Intelligence.

S: Then please explain it to me, my Master.

M: The world views intelligence as imbibing "facts" and "know-how's." If a boy does well in school, he is deemed "intelligent." Is this not the case?"

S: This is the case.

M: But what is taught in schools are the words of others. What is taught in schools is who fought which war in which year. What is taught in school is the process by which to do a mathematical equation. Or memorize facts. Tell me, my student. Of what value are such things to a man's life?

S: Practically speaking, they are of little value, Master.

M: Then if a man contains something within his brain that is of Little Value, how is it that a designation such as "intelligence" can be bestowed upon him?

S: Please continue, Master.

M: If "intelligence" is that act of containing numerous facts, then an encyclopedia must be deemed the most intelligent entity in existence. Is this not so, my student?

S: Yes, Master.

M: But have you ever known anyone to call an encyclopedia "intelligent?"

S: No, Master.

M: If an individual is deemed "intelligent" because he recites facts from textbooks, then it must also be stated that he is less intelligent than the textbooks from which he learns the information. For the textbooks have more facts and information than he does. Is it not so?

S: Yes, Master. But throughout the world, individuals must get a degree in order to plow their trade.

M: Certainly, if they wish to plow a trade, they may procure a degree. But what does this have to do with "intelligence," my dear student?

S: Do you not believe a Doctor to be intelligent, Master?

M: My dear student, the reason that you ask this question is because you are acutely aware of the immense knowledge that doctors hold within their brains. And that they have knowledge that others in society do not. But the same can be said of engineers and computer technicians and attorneys and carpenters and scientists and pilots and so on. And each of these individuals has a knowledge of their domain that others do not. Is this not so?

S: Yes, Master.

M: But if knowledge were intelligence, then any man with an equal amount of knowledge would be deemed equally intelligent.

S: Yes.

M: But is this so? Although two doctors or pilots or engineers may have gone to the same school and read the same textbook, one may be far superior to the other in the execution of his craft. Do we not see this phenomenon all around the world?

S: Yes, Master, this is so.

M: Then this must mean that one of these men has something that the other does not. Correct?

S: Correct.

M: But if the two of them read the same books and listened to the same lectures from the same teacher. And if each of them made the same grades and graduated with high honors, then we can logically assume that they do not differ in their level of Knowledge. Is this so?

S: Yes, Master.

M: But if one is superior to the other in the execution of his craft, then that man must have procured something that the other has not. And that Something must be more than simply Knowledge.

S: What is that Something, Master?

M: That, my student, is Intelligence. Intelligence is not Knowledge. Intelligence is not the accumulation of facts. Intelligence is not following instructions. Intelligence is not procuring a degree or becoming certified or passing an exam.

S: Then what is this thing called Intelligence, Master?

M: Intelligence, my dear student, is something that is attained by way of Instinct rather than Knowledge.

S: Why is this the case, Master?

M: Because you see, my student, Intelligence comes from a place beyond the human mind. And it comes to a man by way of Availability moreso than by "study" or " hard work."

S: I do not understand, Master.

M: When a man has a genuine desire to know The Truth, he deems himself available to knowing it. And thus the Universe infuses it into his bloodstream.

S: I see.

M: My dear student, while the legions of men have spent their lives learning how to cup their hands so that they may carry a few ounces of water, the wise man searches for the Ocean. And once he has found it, he need never carry water again.

S: Thank you, my Master.

MASTER, ARE YOU HAPPY?

Student (S). Master (M).

S: Master, may I ask you a question?

M: Yes.

S: Are you happy, Master?

M: No, my student.

S: Why not?

M: Why should I be happy?

S: I do not understand, Master.

M: What will I do with happiness, my student?

S: What will you do with happiness?

M: Yes. Please tell me, student. What will I do with happiness?

S: You will be happy with happiness.

M: What is the need to be happy?

S: Would you rather be sad?

M: Do you ever see me sad, my student?

S: No.

M: Then can it be settled that sadness must not be the opposite of happiness?

S: Yes. But every man wants happiness.

M: It is so.

S: Why is it that you do not?

M: For the first part of my life, I too chased happiness. But then one day, I saw through the game.

S: The game?

M: You see, my dear student, happiness is a chase. And nothing more.

S: But it is a worthwhile chase, is it not?

M: Perhaps you should ask those who chase it. If they feel that chasing happiness has made them happy, then perhaps it is worthwhile for them.

S: What about you?

M: I have discovered that to chase happiness is to chase a ghost.

S: I've never heard anyone say such a thing, Master. Every man in the world is chasing happiness. Myself included.

M: I understand, my student.

S: But you think I'm wasting my life in doing so?

M: It is not my wish to tell you what to do, my student. Examine the nature of your journey. Have a stark look at what your beliefs have brought you. And decide for yourself.

S: But I'd like your opinion, Master.

M: I try not to have opinions, my student.

S: Then what do you believe about this topic?

M: You will think me difficult, but I do not have any need for belief. I subscribe only to The Truth. And this Truth comes by way of a nuanced and uncompromising exploration of my experiences. I have no interest in resorting to "opinion" or "belief." Either I know or I do not know. If I know, I know. If I do not know, I explore and I experiment until I know.

S: And what you have come to know is that happiness is not the way?

M: What I have come to know is that chasing happiness is to forever hope for circumstances to go your way. But the circumstances are often not in our control. Therefore, we are bound to remain unhappy. And because we are bound to remain unhappy, we get stuck in this chase for happiness. It is a merry-go-round, my student. This is what I have learned.

S: Then what you are saying is to live in the present? Is this your message?

M: Telling a man to "live in the present" is like telling him to scale the north face of Everest with his bare hands. It is silly advice.

S: But do you not live in the moment, Master?

M: My dear student, I live in the moment because I have Discovered it. Not because someone told me to live in it.

S: What is wrong with someone telling you to do so?

M: Because if you do it in such an Insincere fashion, it will never happen. It must come from your heart. You must discover it through Genuineness. It can only be discovered by way of Sincerity.

S: If you do not chase happiness, then what is it that you live for, Master?

M: It has taken me many years to learn what Living really is, my student. I have slowly abandoned the idea of living FOR something. I seek rather to Experience.

S: Experience?

M: Yes, my lovely student. It is all about The Experience.

S: Thank you, my Master.

MASTER, WHAT ARE THE TRUTHS YOU HAVE LEARNED?

Student (S). Master (M).

S: Master, in all of these years of living, what is it that you have learned?

M: I have learned that thought is a liar.

I have learned that feeling is closer to truth.

I have learned that human beings chase and chase, until their lives are no more.

I have learned that there are many places to visit, but nowhere to go.

S: Master, what allowed you to learn?

M: The relentlessness of life. The unforgiveness of nature. The insatiable momentum of the mind. The endless pains.

S: Master, how long did it take for you to succeed?

M: Failure is largely a myth, my student. For anything that is pursued with Sincerity does not fail. And anything that is pursued with hope always fails. My failures were not a failure to achieve. My failures were a failure of cultivating Sincerity before embarking upon The Great Journey.

S: Master, what is your life like now?

M: The way that it should be.

S: Would you please explain?

M: My life is no longer "my life." It is a Living.

S: What is meant by Living, Master?

M: Living, my student, can only occur once one is free of the Mind. Living can only happen once he has crawled out from under its thumb. Therein lies a man's Freedom.

S: What allowed you to crawl out from under the Mind, Master?

M: Desperation. And Sincerity.

S: Will I also be able to climb out from under the Mind, Master?

M: I do not know, my student.

S: Why not, Master?

M: If you seek a prediction from me, the chances are not good.

S: Then what shall I do?

M: When desperation hits you, come to me.

S: And if desperation does not hit me?

M: Then you will live a pitiable life. You will live the life of a prisoner. And you will never become Free.

S: Does it take a lifetime, Master?

M: No, my student.

S: How long does it take?

M: A fraction of a second.

S: Then I am ready, Master.

M: I think not, my student.

S: Why not?

M: Because desperation has not yet risen within you.

S: When will desperation arise, Master?

M: When life becomes unbearable. When you can no longer bear the weight of the mind. When Freedom is the only choice that remains for you. It is then that desperation will arise.

S: You have learned a great deal, Master.

M: Yes, I came to understand Life. But only after I had wasted more than half of it.
For as long as I have breath in these lungs, never shall I waste another day.

S: Thank you, my Master.

MASTER, WHAT DOES IT MEAN TO SEE?

Student (S). Master (M).

M: You must open your eyes.

S: My eyes are open, Master.

M: If only this were true.

S: I do not understand.

M: Do you see the wind?

S: How can one see wind?

M: Do you see what you have done?

S: What is it I have done?

M: Do you see what you have failed to see?

S: What have I failed to see?

M: Do you still believe your eyes are open, my student?

S: How do I open my eyes, Master?

M: Why do you wish to open them?

S: So that I may see.

M: What is it that you wish to see?

S: I do not know.

M: Then they will not open.

S: Have your eyes always been open, Master?

M: No, my student.

S: Is that so?

M: Yes, my student. There was a time when my eyes were as closed as yours. And yet I insisted that they were open.

S: Why, Master?

M: Because at that time I was not a Master. I was a fool.

S: What caused you to see?

M: The stark recognition that I was a fool.

S: How did you come to realize that, Master?

M: I began to suspect it when life never ceased being a struggle.

S: Isn't life always a struggle?

M: Yes, my student. For fools, life can only be a struggle.

S: What did you do when you discovered that your life never ceased to be a struggle?

M: There was nothing to be done.

S: Then how did you come to see?

M: Recognizing that my life never ceased to be a struggle. And recognizing that this could not be The Way were the realizations that began to open my eyes.

S: And when your eyes opened, did everything seem beautiful?

M: Something is "beautiful" only within a background of ugliness. I saw what Was.

S: I do not understand, Master.

M: Do not allow your mind to drift toward romantic illusions, my student.

S: Yes, Master. But please tell me what you saw the day your eyes opened.

M: I saw The Truth. And the truth needs no beauty to enhance it.

S: What was this Truth?

M: How can words possibly carry its weight?

S: You must give me Something, Master.

M: I have given you something, my student.

S: What is that?

M: I have told you that your eyes are closed. And at the moment, this is your greatest Truth.

S: And yet you do not tell me how to open them.

M: My dear student. If I told you how to open them, they would forever remain closed.

S: Why is this so, Master?

M: Because you would forever be lost in an attempt to open them. And your entire life would pass you by.

S: Then what shall I do?

M: Live with the knowledge that your eyes are closed. And when that knowledge makes its way from your head to your heart, your eyes will slowly begin to open.

S: One last question, my Master.

M: Yes, my student.

S: What is the first thing I will see when my eyes open?

M: You will see how pitiable your life was, having lived with your eyes closed.

S: Thank you, my Master.

MASTER, I AM BESET BY PROBLEMS

Student (S). Master (M).

S: I am beset by problems, Master. I suffer all sorts of emotional upheaval. But you do not. Why?

M: How many years it has taken you to ask such a question.

S: Because now I am desperate.

M: I see.

S: Please tell me.

M: Desperation is good because it ensures you will listen. On the other hand, it is not so good, because you may listen too well.

S: I do not understand, Master.

M: Because you are desperate, you will reach out and grab what I throw your way. In a way that you have never been willing to do before. But each thing that I throw to you, you will do it and "see if it works." This will not allow you to see.

S: Then what shall I do, Master?

M: You see? You have started already.

S: What have I done?

M: You ask me for a prescription.

S: But I do not know what else to do.

M: I respected the genuineness of your original statement. You said, 'I suffer all sorts of emotional upheaval. But you do not. Why?'

S: Yes, that is what I wish to know.

M: And yet you dishonor this genuine sentiment by asking for a prescription.

S: My apologies. Please tell me why you do not suffer emotional upheaval, Master.

M: Because I do not give it a reason to come.

S: And I do?

M: You must.

S: But how do you know?

M: Because it comes.

S: Can it not come of its own accord?

M: Can rain come without the invitation of the cloud?

S: I suppose not.

M: You suppose?

S: It is just that . . . I do not know how I give it a reason to come to me.

M: Every creature in nature continually returns to the place they feel at home. Like a bee to nectar. Emotional upheaval feels at home in you. And you feel at home in it.

S: But why would I do such a thing?

M: It is not a question of logic.

S: But there must be more, Master.

M: There is.

S: Please tell me, Master.

M: I am afraid I cannot.

S: But why!

M: The time is not right.

S: When will the time be right?

M: When you are not so desperate to know.

S: But what is wrong with desperation?

M: It will cause you to listen too well.

S: What do you mean by that?

M: I can tell you exactly why your emotional upheaval comes. I can go far deeper than I have. But you see, my dear student, if I

98

do so you will try to eliminate the thing which is causing it.

S: What is wrong with doing so?

M: If I tell you that your emotional upheaval is from Desiring, then you will try to eliminate desire. And in trying to eliminate desire, you will be fighting an uphill battle. And thus you will go nowhere.

S: I see. I can no longer live in emotional upheaval. Nor can I ask you what I should do. Because the prescription will keep me imprisoned to the chase.

M: That is correct, my wise student.

S: But why do others give prescriptions, Master?

M: Because they have not understood the subtle nature and workings of the human mind.

S: But I feel that I am stuck. I cannot stay where I am. Nor can I seek your help in going somewhere else.

M: I understand, my dear student. Come again in the morning. And perhaps your desperation will have begun to heal. And when your mind is not looking, I will whisper to you a quiet

99

and gentle Truth.

S: Yes, my Master.

M: All will be conquered, my dear student. You will arrive at the place you were meant to go. Nature would not have it otherwise. But we will move delicately through the forest of the mind. So as not to snap a twig or rustle the leaves. Lest the mind hear our footsteps.

S: Yes, my Master.

MASTER, WHAT IS LIFE?

Student (S). Master (M).

S: Master, speaking of human beings, what exactly is Life?

M: Life, my student, is Pain.

S: Pain?

M: Yes.

S: How so?

M: Are you not a human being, my student?

S: Yes I am, Master.

M: In all the years that you have lived, have you experienced more joy or more pain?

S: I suppose I never looked at it in such a way. I always looked at it in a way of trying to improve.

M: All human beings do the very same, my student. They try to improve. They try to become happier. They try to become more successful. They try to become healthier. They try to become wiser. They try to become better parents. They try to become better spouses. They try to make more money. And so on.

S: What is wrong with that, Master?

M: My dear student, have you ever seen a Tree try to improve? Or a flower? Or a cloud? Or a bird? Or even the animal who roams the great forest?

S: No, Master.

M: Indeed. Man lives in a perpetual state of Not Knowing. He lives in a perpetual state of Not Understanding. And thus he suffers. And oh how he suffers. His entire existence is mired by one pain after another. And his entire life is devoted to endless attempts at freeing himself from that pain.

S: Did you also suffer, Master?

M: Greatly.

S: Do you suffer now, Master?

M: No, my student.

S: How did you escape? What did you discover?

M: I discovered that my life was suffering. And that no matter what I tried, this suffering would never cease. Rather than trying to improve my condition or to become happier, I decided to go on a Journey to discover the roots of my suffering.

S: The Buddha said that the cause of suffering is craving.

M: The Buddha is correct. But this message will not be understood by Man. For man needs an understanding that is more Immediate, more acute, more relatable to his everyday affairs.

S: What is this understanding, Master?

M: In order for a Man to truly cure anything, he must come face to face with the full gravity of the problem. For it is only then that a Sincere Motivation arises in his heart.

S: And what is the gravity of the problem that he must see, Master?

M: Not every man will be willing to see such a thing. But a few certainly will. He must recognize that his life is fundamentally Pain. And that all his efforts at "happiness" only lead him further into that pain. He must understand that no matter what he tries, whether it is meditation or psychotherapy or medications or support from friends, such things will not have the power to cure his pain. All efforts will be futile. This is what he must understand. And he must understand it deep within his heart.

S: And if he does not?

M: Then he will be like the dog that forever chases its tail.

S: Why does the dog chase its tail, Master?

M: Because it does not understand that the tail was not designed to be caught.

S: And as for man?

M: Man chases "happiness." But in actuality, he doesn't chase happiness at all. He chases freedom from pain. And he believes that happiness is the opposite of pain. And it is this that sinks him. He chases and hopes for "positive events," something to go his way, so that he can gain a moment of happiness. But he does not understand that no matter how many such moments he receives, they are mere drops that punctuate his ocean of pain. Any man should ask himself, In the last 24 hours, how much True Joy did he experience? How about 48 hours? Or 72 hours? Or two months? Or twenty years? It is all pain, my dear student. A man's life is saturated by Pain.

S: Is this why you walked The Path, my Master?

M: Becoming a Master is not a lofty thing, my student. Nor is it noble. Or spiritual. Or religious. It is Practical. It is a Necessity. To Truly Know. To experience The Real Truth. To Understand. So that one may be Free. Is this not what every man truly seeks?

S: Indeed, Master.

M: However, their heads are filled with lofty ideas. Images of flowing robes and living in caves, and head-shaved ascetics. Such things are nonsense. Neither a flowing robe or living in a cave or shaving one's head brings one The Truth. If one chooses to do such things, it is perfectly fine. But the True Master is the one who Understands Life. Who understands why the things that befall him, befall him. The Master is one who is Unperturbed. Who is a leader of men without harboring the slightest interest in leading them.

S: This is indeed what I seek to be, Master. This is most certainly what I seek to become.

M: Then do not fall prey to "the world," my student. It is an enormously powerful distraction. And the greatest form of "the world" is your very own Mind.

S: Thank you, my Master.

MASTER, WHY SHOULD I HELP ANYONE

Student (S). Master (M).

S: You have always been practical with me. Please tell me the practical reason that I should help anyone at all.

M: There is consternation in your voice, my dear student.

S: Yes, Master.

M: I would like to hear about the well from which this question sprang.

S: I fear you will consider me unholy, Master.

M: (Laughs). Holiness is a myth, my student.

S: Then shall I come right out and say it?

M: Without an ounce of fear, my student. This master of yours will never judge you.

S: You have helped many people. And in my own way, I have also helped many people. Yet when we need donations for the temple or other such help, no one comes to help us. I am deeply troubled by this, Master.

M: But we also have charged men for our help.

S: It is true. But I feel that we have given men significantly beyond our charges.

M: It must be so. For transactional work is uninspiring. You must give more than what you get. We mustn't just try to help a man simply in exchange for monetary reward. We must absolutely pour our life into him.

S: There is much emotion inside of me, Master. I feel hesitant to voice it, lest I sound crude and undignified.

M: Do not hold back, my student. Roar at your loudest.

S: Very well. Why should we pour our lives into the men who

come to us? Aside from a monetary sum, THEY do not go out of their way for US. Why should WE do so for THEM? Why should one side go above and beyond, while the other side sticks only to the contract?

M: You are hurt by this, I can see.

S: I am not only hurt by it, Master. I am angered and confused by it. Is man fundamentally selfish and cruel?

M: Selfish, yes. Cruel, no.

S: That is not enough of an explanation for me, Master.

M: I am sympathetic to the way you feel, my student. I have never denied The Truth. And I cannot deny it now. The things that you say are indeed Fact.

S: Then please explain, Master. I beg you, for I feel very strongly about this.

M: Let me first say that as for these men who have Not gone above and beyond to help us as we have to help them, you should know something about them.

S: What is that, Master?

M: It is very likely that they too have gone above and beyond to help others and those others did Not reciprocate them either.

S: I feel like you are trying to soften the blow, Master. Do you hide behind mock rationalism to make me feel better?

M: I rationalize nothing, student. And I have no interest in making you feel better. I speak only The Truth. Such men have very likely not been reciprocated to the degree that they have in their own hearts tried to help others. I cannot say for certain. But it is very likely.

S: That may be so. But what does it change?

M: It is about Understanding, my dear student. It is about seeing things as they are. Seeing human beings as they are.

S: Are human beings fundamentally unkind, Master?

M: Human beings are fundamentally selfish. But not necessarily unkind. Would you like to know why few reciprocate?

S: Yes, Master. I would.

M: Because people are caught up in the momentum of their own lives, student. It is not that they are unkind. It is just that their face is buried so deep in the constant happenings of their own lives that they rarely look up. They do not care about me or you. Nor should they.

S: Forgive me, Master, but then why should I go out of my way to help anyone? Why not just give Exactly according to the monetary sum? Why think about them and consider ways to help them when they are not even in the room? Forgive me, Master, for my emotions, but I want you to answer me straight. No platitudes or spiritual talk. Please tell me head on. Point for point.

M: When have I ever given you platitudes, my student?

S: Forgive me, Master. It is just that I don't want you to deviate from, or soften, the impact of what I'm saying. I beg you to give me real and hard answers to my questions, my Master.

M: I have never shied away from your questions. Nor do I believe in "spiritual" or "feel-good" responses, my student. The hard truth is that no one cares about you. No one cares about me. People only care about themselves.

S: So people are inherently evil?

M: Who mentioned anything about evil? Selfishness is not evil.

111

S: Are all people selfish, Master?

M: The vast majority of people in the world are selfish. Very, very, very few are not. But they do exist.

S: I have yet to see one.

M: And to be honest, you may never see one, my student. As I said, they are as rare as the rarest of gems. But such gems do exist in the world. There are a handful of people in this world like this, but only a handful. Such people perhaps put you and me to shame with their generosity and kindness. Such people are ones whom even I would love to learn from.

S: From where do such rare gems get their kindness and generosity, Master?

M: I do not know, my student. But nature creates gems amidst a sea of pebbles. Such human beings are like the oceans that nourish the rainforests. They are benefactors to humanity. If you give them a drop, they will give you an ocean in return. Not because you ask or hope or even expect (never expect). They do it because it is in their nature to do so.

S: As it is in our nature to give our lives to those whom we help?

M: Precisely. You must understand, my student, that we are not being "nice" by what we do.

S: I do not understand, Master.

M: You and I are Not to be congratulated.

S: How so?

M: Because we are doing things according to our nature. Did the human beings who come to us for help Ask Us to think about them day and night? Did they Ask Us to spend our own time thinking of ways to transform them? We do this of our own accord, my student.

S: Forgive me, Master, but how can you say such a thing? You are almost suggesting that we are to be condemned for spending our days and nights thinking and examining ways to help these human beings?

M: We are not to be condemned. But nor are we to be congratulated.

S: I cannot apologize enough for what I am about to say. But to hell with it all, then, Master.

M: Go on, student. Let it out.

S: I shall just live for myself, then, Master. Perhaps I don't want to help anyone at all!

M: My dear student, do you not receive a monetary sum for your assistance of human beings?

S: Yes.

M: Then you <u>ARE</u> living for yourself.

S: What I mean to say is that I shall do as they do. I will give only as prescribed. I will not go above and beyond. When the person is out of my sights, he will also be out of my mind.

M: Is anyone stopping you from doing this?

S: No.

M: Then do it. Do not try to be benevolent. Understand that whatever you do, the chances of you being Reciprocated beyond the minimum are almost Zero.

S: You paint such a grim picture. But you are correct. It makes me wonder why anyone helps anyone in this world.

M: As I said, no one really helps anyone, my dear and lovely student. They do what is in their Nature to do. If you wish to think about ways to transform someone even when they are not sitting before you, then do it. If you do not, then do not. You are not being "unkind" if you don't. And you are not being "kind" if you do.

S: Then why do it at all?

M: You shouldn't do it. But the reason that you do is because you cannot help yourself. As I cannot help myself.

S: So essentially, become a Martyr, is that it, Master?

M: There is ego in Martyrdom, so do not become a Martyr, my student.

S: I am consumed by confusion, Master.

M: You are confused because you hope. And this hope causes you to question and to strategize.

S: What is the way out of this confusion?

M: To drop all hope.

S: Drop all hope?

M: Yes, my student. Understand that the chances of you encountering A Rare Gem Human Being amidst the common pebbles are akin to you being struck by lightning four times in the same afternoon. If you Understand this, you will drop all hope. And be Free to be as you are.

S: Is this what you do, Master?

M: I have no faith in humanity, my student. Because I understand that humanity is like the sand that shifts with the incoming tide. There is nothing to have faith in. But I do hold close to my heart the Knowledge that somewhere in this world such Gems do exist.

S: But you may never see one.

M: Then I shall Become One, my student. I shall become one.

MASTER, HOW DO I WIN?

Student (S). Master (M).

S: Master, when I fight with a spear, or in hand to hand combat, or even in a running race, how is it that I can assure a win?

M: Why is it that you seek to win, student?

S: That is the purpose of such things. Why else would one play?

M: Do as you will, my student.

S: Meaning?

M: If the reason that you play is to win, I will not try to dissuade you.

S: Do you not play to win, Master?

M: I could go into such things, student. But it will only lead you toward a mass of questions.

S: Please, I truly seek to know, Master. Do you not play to win?

M: I do not.

S: Why, Master?

M: Such things no longer hold any significance for me?

S: Do you, then, play to lose, Master?

M: Winning and losing are, for me, one and the same.

S: Are you implying the old adage, It is not whether you win or lose, but how you play the game?

M: I do not know what this adage means.

S: Do you like to play?

M: It is my duty to play.

S: And when you play, you do not seek to win?

M: No.

S: Why?

M: Student, if I played to win, I would not be able to play.

S: I do not understand, Master.

M: The only one who can truly Play is the one who is indifferent to winning and losing. He who plays to win suffers the wrath of the mind.

S: When did you learn this, Master?

M: I learned this from years of turmoil, my student. There was a time that I not only sought to win, but to crush my opponent. And as sure as I stand before you, those were the most tumultuous years of my life.

S: Did you win often?

M: I won my share. But the price I paid for the win turned out to be too high a price for me.

S: How so, Master?

M: When I played to win, I lost my Freedom. I was filled with angst. I was fully invested in hope. Hoping, at each turn, that fortune would turn away from my opponent, and toward me. While winning did produce a pleasant feeling within me, it was fleeting. But more importantly, I could not forget the imprisonment I felt during the hours of the battle. I shall never go there again.

S: Go where, Master?

M: Toward any ideology that causes me to lose my Freedom. Never again will I stray from that which I hold dearest. The Mind is a voracious animal, my student. It will eat you alive.

S: Shall I no longer train?

M: Why would you no longer train?

S: If I do not seek to win, then what is the point of training?

M: This is a statement born of ignorance, my student.

S: Why, Master?

M: Only the fool trains in order to win. The wise man trains in order to forge his Spirit. He trains in order to perfect his skill. For his craft is his life. And its refinement is his Journey. A Journey toward perfecting himself.

S: I did not realize this, Master.

M: You see, my student. Sport and craft are a vehicle for perfecting oneself. The Legend is not the one who prevails in battle. For any fool can secure a win. The Legend is the one who fights without an ounce of Fear. For he has nothing to lose. The Legend is the one whose heart does not increase its tempo. The Legend is the one who trains his skill in order to forge his spirit, so that neither nature nor misfortune can so much as lay a hand upon him.

S: That sounds incredible, Master. How is it that a man can train in such a way?

M: First comes intention. Then comes training.

S: Intention, Master?

M: Yes. Training is of no use until one has the Sincere Intention to achieve such a thing. When a man Genuinely values his Freedom above all else, then he is Ready.

S: I must confess, Master. I am perhaps not worthy as of yet.

121

M: Your honesty is commendable, student.

S: But I would like to be. Is there a way that I can hasten such readiness?

M: In time, you will come to see. Losses will scar you. Close battles will make you nervous. Anxiety will wrap its tentacles around you.

S: Master, I must admit that such things have already happened to me. Yet I still seem to value winning over Freedom.

M: Perhaps it will happen in this lifetime, student. Or perhaps in the next. Such a Journey appeals to very few men.

S: Why does it appeal to very few men, Master?

M: I do not have an answer for this, my student. I do not have an answer for why a path to Freedom captures the heart of so few men. Perhaps it is Karmic. Perhaps otherwise. I can only say that never in all my life shall I stray from this path.

S: Thank you, my Master.

MASTER, WHAT TRULY IS DEPRESSION?

Student (S). Master (M).

S: Master, what is this thing called Depression?

M: It has come to be modern man's natural state.

S: They say that millions upon millions are depressed. Yet I have not seen many that are depressed.

M: Neither you nor they understand The Truth about depression. The medical establishment sees only one face of depression. And both you and they fail to see the True face of depression.

S: Who do you know that is depressed, Master?

M: I have yet to meet a man or a woman who Is Not depressed.

S: Truly?

M: Truly.

S: But I too see the men and women who come to see you. They seem normal functioning. However, you say that every one of them is depressed?

M: Every one of them.

S: I do not understand, Master.

M: I shall explain this to you on many levels, my student. Firstly, trust not the face that man shows to the world. He has had much practice in concealing himself. He projects a certain image to the world, yet this image is vastly different in the quiet of his home.

S: Please continue, Master.

M: Depression is not only sadness and lack of energy and suicidal thoughts. It is living under the weight of the mind.

S: Under the weight of the mind, Master?

M: Indeed. Each and every man who lives under the weight of the mind suffers an ongoing and incessant undercurrent of turmoil.

His daily life consists of worry, fear, irritability, and concern. He lives in uncertainty. He lives with an unstable mood. He suffers conflicts. He succumbs to anger. His heart races with the subtlest thing that does not go his way. Such is the poison of depression.

S: But the medical world does not define depression in this way.

M: Why would they, student?

S: I do not understand.

M: The medical establishment sees "patients." It does not see human beings. It treats "disease." It knows not of Ease or Dis-ease.

S: In that sense, it is certainly true that every man lives in dis-ease.

M: Man has little choice but to live in dis-ease.

S: Why?

M: Because he lives his life from within the mind. Thus he lives under its weight. And, therefore, he is depressed. He continually is assaulted by the mind. He is a slave. He is constantly bombarded by the shrapnel of involuntary thoughts. He knows

125

not a moment's Peace, my student. He knows not a moment's Peace.

S: But if you were to ask such a man about this, he would tell you this is normal.

M: He would be correct. It is indeed normal. As I said, it has become modern man's natural state. Never trust a man who tells you that he isn't depressed. Do not argue with him. Simply nod your head and smile.

S: Why shall I not tell him that he is depressed?

M: Because if you do he will insist that he is not. His definition of depression will be that which the medical establishment has put forth. He does not even realize that he is depressed. It would be improper for you to disturb a man. Unless he comes forward and asks for help, leave him be, student. As it is said, never try to awaken a sleepwalker.

S: What is a common habit of one who is depressed?

M: Alcohol consumption.

S: Alcohol?

M: Yes. Only a depressed man could invent such a thing. And only a depressed man chooses to consume it.

S: Why, Master?

M: Why does man drink alcohol, my student?

S: Some will say they drink socially. Or because they enjoy the taste.

M: This may be what they have convinced themselves of. But understand dear student, that alcohol is consumed in order to escape the pain of the mind. Man craves an altered state. Because the one that he continually finds himself within is far too turbulent. Alcohol has been become man's answer to the pain of the mind.

S: How does one free himself from alcohol, Master?

M: Free himself? Why on earth would he wish to free himself from alcohol?

S: Because of all of the disastrous consequences. Many of which lead to an early death.

M: Understand this, student. For I will say it softly. Some will admit this to another, while others would not admit it even to themselves. On some level, man seeks to end his life. Understand, dear student, the pain and anxiety and turmoil and depression that man lives under each and every day of his life. Each and every day. Why would he possibly wish to free himself from a substance that would at least temporary shield him from such a painful existence?

S: But some do get treatment for alcohol.

M: This typically happens when one has done something so shameful that he cannot face himself any longer unless he stops drinking. Something catastrophic, or on the verge of catastrophe. The decision to abandon the elixir that gives a man a temporary relief from the pain of his mind will not be made casually.

S: Thus, alcohol is inevitable for most people?

M: Rare is the man who does not consume alcohol. And the only way that he would stop is if the pain of the mind began to cease. Then he would not have anything to have a respite from. In fact, his daily life would become a heaven, rather than a hell.

S: Then such things should be explained to people.

M: My dear student, how many sermons do you hear all around

the world? From the pulpit to the living room. Man does not listen to other men. Unless he arrives at a state in which he is Truly Ready to walk a new path. When his current way of living is no longer acceptable to him, he will come. And he will come of his own accord. You will not have to convince him. You will find him on your doorstep. So that you may show him The Way that he seeks. The Way To Freedom. Freedom from the pains of the mind.

S: Thank you, my Master.

MASTER, WHAT IS MY POTENTIAL?

Student (S). Master (M).

S: Master, I have heard you speak of the potential of human beings. Please tell me, Master. What is my potential?

M: You know not what you ask, student.

S: Why, Master?

M: What if I told you that your potential was very limited? That you would only amount to such and such, and never anything more?

S: Is this the Truth, Master?

M: What if it were?

S: Then I would be disturbed.

M: And what if I told you that your potential was glorious. That you would ascend to the greatest of heights, higher than any man before you?

S: Do you toy with me, Master?

M: I am asking you a question, student.

S: If that were my potential, then I would be pleased.

M: Therefore, whether you are disturbed or pleased is entirely dependent upon my words. You have placed not only your trust, but the whole of your future in my hands. Your entire potential can be made or unmade with a few words from my lips.

S: You are, then, saying that it is a foolish question.

M: That is for you to decide, student.

S: But you are no ordinary man, Master. You know The Truth.

M: Student, what good is any Truth that destroys the will of a human being?

S: Will it my destroy my will?

M: You have said that you would feel disturbed if I stated that your potential was limited.

S: You are correct.

M: You see, my student, man has a habit of asking non-questions. He states phrases in a question's cloak.

S: I do know, however, that my personality is one of determination. I tend not to leave things undone. I have a fairly strong work ethic.

M: Your personality is immaterial, student.

S: Immaterial? How can this be so?

M: Personality has nothing to do with Potential.

S: But a lazy man hasn't the ability to achieve as much success as the hard working man.

M: Both have an enormous potential.

S: How can a lazy man possibly have an enormous potential, Master?

M: Personality affects the execution of each of these men.

S: But the hard working man executes, while the lazy man does not. How can personality affect the hard working man?

M: The lazy man is a sloth. The hard working man is a mule. There is little qualitative difference between them.

S: You do not value hard work, Master?

M: The world sees nobility in hard work. I do not.

S: Then what is it that you see nobility in, Master?

M: Truth. Understanding. Clarity.

S: And such things do not come from hard work?

M: Such things come from a desire to Know. And rare is the man who wishes To Truly Know.

S: Why is this so?

M: Because it is far easier to be slothful or hard working than it is to be a Seeker.

S: A Seeker?

M: Yes, a Seeker of Truth. In any and all domains.

S: That is an interesting idea, Master.

M: Do not follow the ways of the world, student. It is replete with ignorance. It is fascinated by a man who has spent years learning to emit fire from his mouth through hard work. When he could have lit a match in a second. There is no dignity in toil, when the Truth is available. The world believes that man should become effortful so as to achieve the highest result. But tell me student, is it not wiser to find a way to achieve an even greater result with a fraction of the work?

S: You are advocating doing the Least?

M: The fact that you are horrified by this question demonstrates that you've succumbed to the culture. The world would have a man beat himself into the ground, wear his bones thin, regardless of whether he achieves the result. But the ones who Know do a fraction of the work, and achieve infinitely greater results. For their dignity lies in knowing The Truth, rather than aiming for sweat and toil.

S: But parents have for centuries taught their children to never do the minimum. To go the extra mile. To do more than what is expected of them.

M: Certainly. That is because school has no outcome. There is nothing of any practical value to aim for. Therefore, the only thing that remains are empty ideals to turn man into a mule. Doing well in school only gets you more school. It has no life. It has no practical value. But in the real world, creating something has true value. True value to man himself, and to the society in which he creates it. Thus Efficiency is of utmost importance. In school, efficiency has no value, as there is no real consequence. It is a house of cards.

S: What about education?

M: Such big words you use, student. Please enlighten me. What does it mean to be "educated?"

S: I confess, I have never been asked such a question before, Master.

M: To the world, education is to memorize and recite a litany of irrelevant facts. What year such and such war occurred. Trigonometry. World history. What is a participle? Of what use are such things to the lives of human beings? How can such a thing be called education?

S: I do not know, Master.

M: To be Educated means to Know something of value. To Know something that can transform a human life. To advance the life of man in a significant way. His being. His state. His inner condition. Is it not nonsensical? Rather than transforming the inner condition of man in order to prevent wars, humans are asked to go to "school" in order to relive and recite the details of the wars that have taken place.

S: I understand, Master. What, then, is the ultimate potential of a human being?

M: My initial instinct is to explain the incredible potential of human beings. But such things will not penetrate you. Because they are not in your experience.

S: Then please tell me what a man can do in order to have such an experience.

M: Even listing these things will become prescriptive. And thus you will be certain not to pursue them.

S: I beg you, Master.

M: A man must somehow accumulate a basic level of disgust for the status quo. If he is not disgusted by it, he will become a part of it. He must understand that that which society values is the low and the mediocre. He must be inquisitive enough to wonder what might exist beyond the level of society's norms. He must have a love for attaining Clarity. He must become haunted by what he might not know. Then he has a chance of moving toward his potential.

S: I understand, Master. Before you go, please tell me this. Is it veritably true that I can become absolutely anything that I wish to become?

M: The answer was initially Yes. But now that you have asked the question, it has instantly become No.

S: Thank you, my Master.

MASTER, WHY DO YOU BETRAY ME?

Student (S). Master (M).

S: Master, I must admit that I am troubled by something. I have been troubled by it for some time. I've hesitated in telling you so as not to offend. But I cannot keep it inside any longer.

M: Fear not, my student. Speak freely.

S: If I speak freely, I fear that emotion will get the better of me.

M: It matters not.

S: Master, in some ways I feel that you have betrayed me.

M: Tell me, student. How have I betrayed you?

S: Master, I have given my life to learning from you. I cherish your every word. I long for your teachings. But it seems that you give others more than you give to me?

M: Please explain, student.

S: A few days prior, an old man from the village came to see you. You invited him in. You sat with him for a very long time. He asked questions and you answered his every one. Forgive me, but I overheard. The things that you told him were things that you have never once told me. I feel that you have withheld things from me. This was a simple man from the village. And you gave him so much. I am your own student, and yet it seems you give me small and hesitating doses of teachings.

M: Your suspicions are correct, my student.

S: They are correct? How easily you speak these words, Master. Do you not care about me?

M: How to explain to someone who does not understand?

S: Please try, Master. I beg you.

M: My dear student, is it possible to sit you down before me and reveal to you in succession every Truth about everything in your life? And explain each one thoroughly so that you will be fortified with the Knowledge that few men on this Earth ever come to possess? The answer is Yes.

S: Then, by all means —

M: But having done so, will you understand?

S: I believe so.

M: I believe not, my dear student. I believe not.

S: I am in a fit of frustration, Master.

M: Why is this so, student?

S: Because I stand before a man who can give to me all of the Secrets and the Great Truths of life. Truths that could transform my life entirely within a moment's time. And yet I am unable to convince him to do so.

M: This is not the true fit of frustration, student. The true fit of frustration should be that you stand before a man who can give you these things this very minute. However, even having been given them, you are not ready to hear them. Though you will hear the words, they will not penetrate. They will bounce off of you like metal pellets off of a tin can. They will only spawn
140

endless questions.

S: Then what of that old man who came to see you? You told him many things, did you not?

M: You mentioned that you overheard the conversation.

S: Yes.

M: And having heard some of the Truths, did you understand them?

S: (Sigh). I must confess that I did not. But I hate to confess this, Master.

M: Why?

S: Because this will only justify your decision to withhold these Truths from me.

M: The only man who needs justification is the one who is uncertain.

S: And you will make Certain not to reveal these Secrets to me. You reveal them to an old stranger from the village. But you will not reveal them to your own loyal student.

M: Such things are not given to those who are Loyal. They are given to those who are Ready.

S: And that old man was ready?

M: Yes.

S: Why?

M: You were not of the right mind to hear the questions he asked. The questions that he asked could only have been asked by one who is Ready.

S: How do I become Ready, Master? Please tell me this.

M: Allow me to begin with the first Truth. May I?

S: Please do, Master.

M: The first Truth is this: You are not interested in the Truths, student. You are only interested in hearing them.

S: I do not understand, Master.

M: To you, these Great Truths are not what is most valuable. What is most valuable to you is that you Receive Them. You are more interested in receiving the Gift of Truth, than you are in receiving the Truths themselves. This is why you have become envious of the old man. For he Received them, while you did not.

S: You put me in a bind, my Master. You are not a man I can argue with. Will you at least tell me how I can become Ready?

M: It is not a matter of "how," my student. When a man is Ready, the clouds part. The town bell rings slightly off tune. The air around him grows thick.

S: Forgive me, Master. I do not understand.

M: Your eyes will reveal your readiness, student. For they will seek nothing else. They will be Fixed and Ready. You will have set aside all else in your life. And you will sit and wait. Come high winds or high tide. And at that moment, I will take you by my side and I will reveal to you all the things that Man was meant to know. But few ever do.

S: Yes, my Master. But may your obstinate student beg you for a single Truth, though admittedly he has not shown himself worthy.

M: (Smile). I will grant your request, my student.

S: Thank you, my Master. My eyes and ears belong to you at this moment.

M: Dear student, Every problem in your life exists because you fail to see it for what it truly is. All that you have ascribed it to is incorrect. If you were, for a single moment, able to see these problems for what they Truly were, every one of them would vanish before your next breath.

S: Thank you, my Master.

MASTER, WHY IS MAN'S LIFE FILLED WITH PAIN?

Student (S). Master (M).

S: Master, man's life is filled with endless pain. I can speak firsthand.

M: I assume you mean emotional pain.

S: Yes, Master.

M: The common man's life contains little else, my student.

S: Why is this so?

M: Because he lives his life through ego.

S: How else can a man live his life, if not through ego?

M: He can live his life through wisdom.

S: This is easier said, is it not?

M: Is it easy to live a life of pain, my student?

S: No, Master. It certainly is not.

M: It is a great tragedy that the whole of a man's existence is spent living in pain. Even that which he thinks is fortuitous is also pain. It is a terrible way to live.

S: But few ever find the wisdom to turn away from it. Is this correct, Master?

M: Yes, my student. This is most correct.

S: Is attaining wisdom so difficult that a life of pain is almost certain?

M: It is not that attaining wisdom is so difficult. It is just that man is simply unwilling to separate himself from his ego.

S: Please tell me, Master. If man were to separate himself from his ego would he truly live a life free of pain?

M: He would instantly rid himself of all pain.

S: It is that powerful?

M: Yes.

S: Is such a grand reward not worth the price of a man's ego?

M: It is for me. But I cannot speak for another.

S: It is certainly worth it for every man. Is it not?

M: What you must understand, student, is that in his view, a man's ego is all he has. It is his foundation. It is the place from which he acts, and from which he sees the world. How can one ask him to separate himself from such a thing?

S: Because of what he will get in return. A life free of pain.

M: Firstly, he is not convinced that this will be the natural result. Secondly, the pain that he will endure in separating himself from his ego may be more unbearable to him than an entire life of pain.

S: I do not understand, Master. It seems you are making a convincing case in favor of man remaining firmly within his ego.

M: In the traditions and the ways of the world, men are preached at. They are instructed to do this and that. Whether it is in the name of spirituality, religion, self development, psychotherapy, or otherwise. But I find such things deplorable.

S: Why, Master?

M: Because they look upon man as one who is to be "instructed." You will see that although men may hear such "sermons" and "instructions" and "psychologizing", few follow them. Whether it is in the church pew, the lecture hall, the ashram, the therapist's couch, or the holy gathering.

S: This is true, Master. Then what is the way to talk to men?

M: Man must be understood. He must be respected. Before you ask a man to be wise, the one speaking to him must act in wisdom. He must not instruct. He must look at things from the man's point of view. To simply tell him to become "present" or "egoless" or "kind" or "compassionate" is not only unwise, it is silly. It is just silly.

S: Are you, then, saying that you support man's reluctance to separate himself from his ego?

M: I do not support it. I understand it. If in his eyes a man views his ego as part and parcel of himself, he will not let it go. No matter what holy figure asks him to do so. It is not about "instructions." It is about understanding.

S: Then you are essentially saying that man is doomed to a life of pain.

M: If you look at the billions of humans that inhabit this earth, you will see that this is precisely the case. There is no need to predict or forecast. Simply look around you and you will see that this is precisely what is happening. And it has been happening for centuries.

S: Does any man stand a chance of living a life free of pain, Master? Or are they all doomed?

M: The fact is that almost all are doomed. But there is the rare man who will consider it.

S: Why would he consider it while the others do not?

M: There are many reasons. Too many to explain. But, for one, his unwillingness to continue living a life of pain.

S: But will this man not feel pain when separating himself from his ego, as the others do?

M: It is not whether or not this separation will be painful. It is whether he feels that this pain will be lesser or greater than an entire life of pain.

S: And this is something he will have to weigh?

M: That is correct.

S: Was it painful for you to separate yourself from ego, Master?

M: It was somewhat painful, but frightening moreso.

S: Frightening, Master?

M: Yes. Like a ship without a rudder.

S: Then why did you carry it through, Master?

M: Because the alternative was no longer acceptable.

S: The alternative being a life of pain?

M: Pain. Turmoil. Emotional attachment. Swings of mood. Constant and endless anxiety. All manner of internal strife. I no longer had use for such things.

S: And now such turmoil is no longer a part of your life?

M: That is correct.

S: It must feel wonderful, Master.

M: In the beginning it feels wonderful. Because the memories of the old life remain fresh. They remain as a dark background against this new found Freedom. But after a while, this becomes one's normal way of living. It is neither wonderful nor ecstatic. It simply is.

S: Thank you, my Master.

MASTER, HOW DO I ATTAIN INNER QUIET?

Student (S). Master (M).

S: Master, I am desperate to have quiet. I have sought it for a long time. But it constantly eludes me.

M: I assume you mean quiet in the mind.

S: Yes, Master. I am tormented by thoughts. And worries. And anxieties. And fears. And disappointments. It never ends, Master. It simply never ends.

M: Yes.

S: Please help me.

M: What sort of help would you like, my student?

152

S: I will leave that to your good wisdom, Master.

M: What I essentially hear you saying is that you would like Me to make you quiet.

S: I want to become quiet. Once and for all. I seek any guidance that you are able to provide, Master.

M: I have no "doing" if that is what you seek.

S: Whatever you have I will happily take, Master. For desperation stands at my door.

M: May I ask you a question, my student?

S: Yes, Master.

M: Why is it that you do not have Quiet, my student?

S: I do not know, Master. Please tell me.

M: It is because you seek selective Quiet.

S: I do not understand, Master.

M: When things are in disarray, you seek Quiet. And when things are fortuitous, you do not.

S: So I should not become happy by fortuitous events?
M: There is no "should."

S: Forgive me, Master. Yes, of course.

M: Life is designed in a particular way. The Mind is designed in a particular way. You must take it all. Or leave it all. But selectivity is to introduce duality. And duality is the lifeblood of the mind that torments you.

S: So this is the choice before me?

M: In a way, yes. But to a man of wisdom, it is hardly a choice at all.

S: How so, Master?

M: Because the man of wisdom has seen enough. He has had enough. And he will be fooled or tempted no more.

S: Would you kindly explain, Master?

M: The man of wisdom has seen that all joys are followed by misery. All pleasures are followed by pain. He has seen the undeniable reproducibility of this fact. And thus he has grown tired of seeking pleasure. And in so doing he has become immune to the pain that follows.

S: And this man of wisdom attains quiet how?

M: He does not need to attain it at all. It becomes his.

S: Why does it become his?

M: Because he has relinquished the causes, he no longer suffers the effects. If you are no longer interested in "good" things, "bad" things cannot disturb you.

S: But practically, is it not impossible to no longer be interested in "good" things, Master?

M: Not if you see that five bad things follow each good one. It doesn't require an overly intelligent or "spiritual" individual to see this. It requires only an observant one.

S: Master, may I ask you a question?

M: Yes, my student.

S: Do you truly no longer hope for good things to happen to you?

M: My dear student, the greatest thing that can possibly happen to me has already happened.

S: What is that, Master?

M: The Freedom from the need to seek anything.

S: But what about practices, skills, work, art, and so forth?

M: Certainly, I continue to refine those things. But the refinement is the joy. Not the hope that something "good" will come from it.

S: But if nothing "good" comes from it, then the refinement is a waste, is it not?

M: No.

S: Why not?

M: Because if it does not bring about a glorious and consistent result, then it means I have not yet found The Truth. So I continue to refine.

S: And the glorious Truth of achieving quiet within me will come of its own accord?

M: The Truth always comes of its own accord.

S: Then I suppose I must wait patiently for it.

M: Certainly not.

S: Then must I work for it?

M: Certainly not.

S: Then what must I do, Master?

M: As I said, there is no "doing."

S: Please show a bit of compassion, Master.

M: I tease you not, my student. I must speak Truth, whether it aids you are frustrates you.

S: But if I neither Wait nor Work for it, then what is The Way?

M: The Way is not a map. It is a Quality.

S: A Quality, Master?

M: Yes. A quality of observation, keen discrimination, and

157

interior examination. If you Wait, you will be a beggar who deserves nothing. If you Work, you will be a mule who attains nothing. You must seek to Understand, student. Understand the patterns of your life that have repeated themselves over and over again. And this understanding is borne of astute and incisive observation. And this astute and incisive observation is borne of the Genuine Desire to be immune to all things that life has to offer. Most especially the "good" things.

S: Thank you, my Master.

MASTER, PLEASE TELL ME ABOUT GOD

Student (S). Master (M).

S: Master, I have never heard you speak of God. Why is this so?

M: What would you like to know, student?

S: Is there a God?

M: The answer to this question will not help you.

S: But I would really like to know if such a thing as God exists.

M: What are your thoughts on this topic, student?

S: When I was a little boy, there was a holy man who wandered through our village. He would sing songs about God. He would

159

praise him day and night. He would tell us that God would look out for us in our lives.

M: Perhaps one day I shall speak with this holy man.

S: Yes. I would love to see you do so. Please tell me your thoughts, Master.

M: Let us take your life as an example, my student.

S: Yes, Master.

M: Has your life been filled with happiness, peace, and freedom?

S: No, Master. It has not.

M: And if a God existed, and if he were looking out for you as this holy man said, why would your life lack happiness, peace, and freedom?

S: I do not know. Perhaps if there is a God, he has rules. And if one does not know the rules, he does not receive God's blessings.

M: Perhaps you are correct, student. But does not the whole of humanity live in pain, disappointment, sadness, and misery?

S: Yes, Master. It does.

M: Then, according to your logic, virtually no one on Earth must know God's rules.

S: Perhaps so.

M: And if no one knows God's rules, of what use is God? Whether he exists or not.

S: I understand, Master. But may I ask you a question?

M: Yes.

S: Do you truly know if God exists or not?

M: No, my student. I do not.

S: And does it trouble you not to know?

M: No.

S: Why not?

M: Whether God exists or not, I do not know. But I do not trouble myself looking for him.

S: Why, Master?

M: Because what will I do if I find him?

S: You might ask him for something.

M: Why should I ask him for something?

S: Why not?

M: Because I do not want anything.

S: I do not know how to respond to that, Master.

M: It seems to me that the only reason human beings wish to know about God is because they want something from him. If it was believed that God did not have the power to give, I do not believe any human being on earth would ever utter his name.

S: What if what they want is peace, happiness, and freedom?

M: If there were a God, would he not know that his children are craving peace, happiness, and freedom?

S: Yes.

M: Then why would he wait to be asked?

S: Does anyone or anything give freely?

M: Certainly.

S: Please explain, Master.

M: Does the sun need to be asked to gives its warmth? Do the rivers need to be asked to quench a man's thirst? Does nature not give itself whole to any and all living creatures, whether they ask or not?

S: Indeed it does, Master.

M: Then if there is a God, why would he wait to be asked to give something that he already knows is desperately needed?

S: I do not know, Master.

M: Nor I, student. Whether a one such as this exists or not, I do not know. If someday I happen to encounter him, I will ask him these questions directly, so that he may dispel my ignorance. But until such time, the only thing that I have is this life within me. That is the only Verifiable Truth that I have.

S: Thank you, my Master.

MASTER, PLEASE GIVE ME THE SECRET TO ENLIGHTENMENT

Master (M). Student (S).

S: You will think this an unfair and childish question, Master. But I want to become Enlightened Today. How can I do so?

M: Your question is a non-starter.

S: Why?

M: Because once a man becomes Enlightened, he loses awareness of himself. But that is not what you are seeking.

S: Then what is it that I am seeking, Master?

M: You are seeking the pleasure that comes from becoming Enlightened.

S: And what is wrong with that?

M: Once a human being becomes Enlightened, there is no one to receive the pleasure.

S: Then what shall I do?

M: About what?

S: About becoming Enlightened.

M: The world has filled you with silly ideas, my student.

S: You don't believe in Enlightenment, Master?

M: Not as an attainment.

S: I am confused.

M: I will help you, my student.

S: How?

M: By ignoring the question you asked, and answering the question you did not.

S: You are going to answer a question that I did not ask?

M: I am going to answer the question that you want to ask but do not know how to ask it.

S: What is that question?

M: Why go to that trouble when I can provide you with a response to it instead?

S: Very well, Master. I am listening.

M: The experience that you seek can be found.

S: How?

M: By choosing to live in Oblivion.

S: Oblivion?

M: Yes.

S: I do not understand, Master.

M: Oblivion can give you what your false notions of Enlightenment cannot.

166

S: What does it mean to live in oblivion, Master?

M: It means to live Oblivious to all that you know in your head, feel in your heart, and see with your eyes.

S: If I live obliviously, how will I be able to function? And to live?

M: With the sort of beauty, grace, and equanimity that you have never before known.

S: But if I become oblivious, I will no longer know anything.

M: You will know Completely and Precisely.

S: But if I become oblivious, I will not see what is around me.

M: You will see for the first time in your life.

S: But if I become oblivious, I will not be able to plan, formulate, and create a life.

M: You will utilize perfectly measured doses of the utilitarian mind in order to achieve all ends you wish to achieve. Without the compulsory emotional turmoil that accompanies them.

S: I suspect there is More to Oblivion than you are letting on.

M: Certainly. But let this be an introduction to this new way of life. For it is a secret passage way to "instant Enlightenment."

S: Thank you, my Master.

MASTER, I AM READY TO RECEIVE THE GREAT TRUTHS

Student (S). Master (M).

S: Master, I am ready.

M: I do not know what to say to you, my student.

S: Why is that, Master?

M: Words cannot express.

S: Your joy?

M: My ambivalence.

S: Ambivalence, Master?

M: Yes.

S: I do not understand, Master.

M: Yes, I truly do not know what to say.

S: I am ready for The Truth, my Master. So why not tell it to me?

M: Where is it that I should begin?

S: The beginning, Master.

M: There is no beginning. All things fold into themselves.

S: Is it that you would rather not tell me? Is this the ambivalence, Master?

M: No. The ambivalence lies in getting across to you the fact that Truths reveal themselves in measured doses. In the realm of experience.

S: Then so be it.

M: I see the innocent look in your eye, and thus I will try. I think at the end of this exchange you perhaps will understand.

S: Truly, Master?

M: Yes. But do not become excited, my student. For the thing that you will perhaps understand is not exactly what you hope to understand.

S: I see. How shall we proceed, Master?

M: Ask any question that you like. And I will answer it. But I will warn you, the answers may not satisfy you. But they will be The Truth. This I can assure you.

S: Very well. Are you ready, Master?

M: Yes.

S: Is there a God?

M: No.

S: What is enlightenment?

M: The holistic dissolution of the self.

S: What is the mind?

M: Ego.

S: How does one achieve happiness?

M: There is no such thing.

S: From where does wisdom arise?

M: Dispassionate observation.

S: How can I have Peace?

M: By living without the mind.

S: How do I learn to love myself?

M: This will only create more problems for you.

S: What is the most important thing in life?

M: Nothing has importance.

S: What is the best way to spend one's life?

M: It depends upon the end one wishes to achieve.

172

S: What is love?

M: Not what you believe it to be.

S: What makes you happy?

M: Nothing.

S: What makes you sad?

M: I do not allow myself the luxury of sadness.

S: What is it that you seek above all else?

M: Vairagya (Dispassion).

S: What is Art?

M: The fingertips having a mind of their own.

S: What does life give to human beings?

M: A steady stream of pain.

S: Is this pessimistic?

M: Yes. For the optimist.

S: Is the optimist not better than the pessimist?

M: There is no difference.

S: How can I help the world?

M: By discovering Yourself.

S: How can world wars be stopped?

M: By dismantling all governments.

S: How to stop world hunger?

M: Man is hungry for something other than food. And once the hungry are sufficiently fed, they will exchange the disease of hunger for the diseases of those who are satiated.

S: Will I become a Master?

M: No.

S: Why not?

M: Because you asked.

S: What is the most dangerous human emotion?

M: Hope.

S: How do we get others to like us?

M: No one cares about You.

S: Truly?

M: Truly.

S: Do you care about me?

M: No.

S: I am saddened, Master.

M: I understand.

S: Do you not have room in your heart for anyone?

M: A pint of blood.

S: Forgive me, but this sounds rather cold.

M: Nothing to forgive.

S: I wish to be with you always. Is this possible?

M: No.

S: Why not?

M: Because I will soon be dead.

S: Is there anything in this world worth living for?

M: No.

S: Then what is the aim of a man's life?

M: To become enlightened.

S: Why?

M: Because the alternative is an endless torrent of misery.

S: What is your idea of enlightenment.

M: A dissolution of the self.

S: Why would anyone choose to dissolve himself?

M: Why would anyone choose to live a life of untold turmoil?

S: What is it that gives you True Satisfaction?

M: I will admit a guilty morsel of pleasure.

S: Please tell me, Master.

M: A handful of True, Authentic, and Genuine students who seek to become True Masters.

S: What does it mean to become a Master.

M: To live a life completely free of even the slightest trace of turmoil.

S: Is such a thing possible?

M: Not for the one who wonders.

S: How did you come to be so uncompromising?

M: This I learned from life. Which is endlessly uncompromising.

S: Fight fire with fire, is it?

M: To finally end the fighting. And see the strings behind the stage.

S: Are you touched by ambition?

M: Unfortunately, to a degree.

S: What is your ambition?

M: My passion for guiding Genuine Seekers.

S: What do you hate?

M: I hate when I allow myself to hate. And when I allow myself to hate, I do so voluntarily, and inadvertently release myself from the hate.

S: What is one particular holy grail that you train yourself to achieve?

M: A beautiful question.

S: One I would love to know the answer to, Master.

M: To arrive at the state in which even the Thought of things to be other than the way they are fail to arise within my mind.

S: Is it possible to have everything?

M: To need nothing is to have everything.

S: What is your default state?

M: Incisive observation into the way things are at this moment.

S: What is fear?

M: The offspring of desire.

S: What is anger?

M: The offspring of hope.

S: Master, I feel as if I need a mountain of explanation for each of these questions.

M: Yes.

S: The Truth is quite complicated.

M: The Truth is simple. The Mind is complicated.

S: That is all for now, Master.

M: May I ask you a question, my student?

S: Yes, Master.

M: What have these Truths done for you?

S: If I may be honest, it is too soon to tell.

M: Very good, my student.

ABOUT THE AUTHOR

If I may be honest, I do not know exactly what it is that I do.

I understand that this is neither fashionable nor "correct." But it is The Truth.

And The Truth is all I have to offer any human being.

In my Journeys with the glorious human beings who, for whatever reason, seek my counsel, there emerges a sort of mysterious alchemy. One that continues to fascinate me.

Whether it is a Professional Athlete, a Celebrity, an Artist, or a CEO, the journey toward a life of Uncompromising Freedom continues.

And whomever I may have transformed in some small measure or fashion, it is I who is transformed time and again

181

by the wisdom of those who I am fortunate to counsel.

My previous book is Atmamun: The Path To Achieving The Bliss Of The Himalayan Swamis And The Freedom Of A Living God.

My Online Presence:

www.KapilGuptaMD.com
www.SiddhaPerformance.com
www.SiddhaPerformanceGolf.com
Twitter: @KapilGuptaMD
Facebook: www.facebook.com/KapilGuptaMD
Email: Kapil@KapilGuptaMD.com

Printed in Poland
by Amazon Fulfillment
Poland Sp. z o.o., Wrocław